# A TASTE OF PARIS

# A TASTE OF PARIS

## TRADITIONAL FOOD

## BY THEODORA FITZGIBBON

Period photographs specially prepared by GEORGE MORRISON

1974 · HOUGHTON MIFFLIN COMPANY BOSTON

First Printing   w

First American Edition
Copyright © 1974 by Theodora FitzGibbon

*Library of Congress Cataloging in Publication Data*
FitzGibbon, Theodora.
A taste of Paris.
1. Cookery, French. 2. Paris—Description—Views.
I. Title.
TX719.F65   1974        641.5′944        74-7499
ISBN 0-395-19393-1

Printed in the United States of America

To Desmond and Mary with love and many thanks for all the 'tastes of Paris' over the years.

# ACKNOWLEDGMENTS

We both want to thank several very good friends who helped us enormously in many ways during the research for this book. Particularly Madame Monique Williams for recipes and for putting us in touch with restaurateurs and other people connected with food in Paris; Mademoiselle Lotte Eisner for introducing us to M. Adhémar of the Cabinet des Estampes, Bibliothèque Nationale, who gave us every assistance; Desmond and Mary Ryan for their most kind hospitality and the loan of books for research.

We also convey our thanks to M. André Hurtrel, President du Comité National de Gastronomie for his kindness and information; Madame Milan of La Closerie des Lilas for photographs, recipes and her valuable time; La Tour d'Argent for an invaluable photograph and recipes; and Madame Vaudable of Maxim's for recipes.

We particularly want to thank M. Montgolfier of the Musée Carnavalet for his courtesy and kindness, and his assistant M. Broyard who went out of his way to find us material. Also the Musée Marmottan for the photograph on page 69. Miss Roisin Kirwan of my local library once again came to my rescue and found me out of print books, for which I am permanently in her debt.

Photographs on pages xii, 3, 5, 7, 10, 12, 16, 20, 23, 24, 39, 40, 43, 47, 50, 55, 57, 61, 63, 64, 66, 70, 73, 75, 77, 78, 83, 84, 86, 89, 91, 92, 94, 98, 101, 102, 107, 109, 111, 113, 115, 116, 118 are reproduced by kind permission of the Musée Carnavalet; on pages 15, 18, 26, 28, 30, 32, 35, 45, 48, 52, 80 by kind permission of the Bibliothèque Nationale, Cabinet des Estampes; on page 69 by kind permission of the Musée Marmottan; on page 8 by courtesy of La Tour d'Argent; on page 104 by courtesy of B.B.C. Hulton Picture Library; and the photograph on page 37 by courtesy of Roger-Viollet. Endpaper photographs by George Morrison by courtesy of the Musée Carnavalet.

# CONTENTS

# INTRODUCTION

Few people would dispute that Paris is the gastronomical capital of the Western world and has been so for several centuries. Apart from the enormous care taken in the preparation of food in France it must also be remembered that its agricultural resources are vast, it being the only country in Europe with climatic temperatures which range from the subarctic in mountainous regions, to extreme heat in the south. It also possesses a northern cold sea coast, Atlantic and Mediterranean waters which account for the large variety of fish and shellfish found all over the country. It is, in fact, self-supporting in food, which is probably the reason for the large number of regional dishes, many of which are served daily in Paris, both in the home and in restaurants. With such a large repertoire available it is not surprising that, unlike cities such as London and New York, the *cuisines* of other countries are in the minority.

Nevertheless, certain foreign queens have left legacies to France: Buontalenti, one of the many chefs brought to France by Catherine de Medici in 1533, delighted the French court with his iced confections which were previously unknown there. At that time Italian head chefs were considered the best in the world and the French cooks had the good sense to learn from them and not to indulge in the rough behaviour of the *rôtisseurs*, who frequently resorted to arms if their rights were infringed. Maria Theresa (1638–83), who was born in Madrid, introduced the Spanish *olla podrida*, *Hors d'œuvre* (from the Spanish *entremeses*), also the arrangement of courses or removes, rather than an immense spread. The Austrian queens brought their Austrian pastry-cooks, who entranced the courtiers with their feather-light cakes. Noble ladies showed the same interest in the preparation of food that the French housewife shows today; the Princesse de Conti is said to have invented the idea of serving lamb with lentils, and the Marquise de Valromey has left us a superb recipe for cooking hare. See page 103.

The preparation and serving of food have always been treated as an art, and it is this approach which makes French food so consistently good. In royal households the carving of meat or poultry was executed by a nobleman, known as *esquire tranchant*, and the last tutor employed to complete a young nobleman's education was a master of carving. This extreme interest which has been manifest in French cooking for so many centuries, is summed up by the great contemporary chef Alexandre Dumaine: 'Pour faire de la bonne cuisine, une femme doit avoir un peu de soin et beaucoup de cœur' – 'to be a good cook, a woman must put a little care and a lot of heart into it. . . .'

I have tried to avoid *haute cuisine* dishes, since they are for professional cooks, but rather to make this book practical and useful for the person who likes to put 'a little care and a lot of heart' into cooking. With so much to choose from, making the selection was difficult, so both visually and literally this book is simply 'A Taste of Paris'.

THEODORA FITZGIBBON 1973

Inis Caoin,
Deilginis,
Baile Átha Cliath.

Inis Caoin,
Dalkey,
Dublin.

x

'The pleasures of the table belong to all ages, to all conditions, to all countries and to every day: they can be associated with all the other pleasures and remain the last to console us for the loss of the rest.'

Jean Anthelme Brillat-Savarin. 1755–1826

# EATING IN PARIS FROM EARLY TIMES

Until the eighteenth century there were no restaurants in Paris (although many had existed in London almost a hundred years earlier), the first one being founded by Antoine Beauvilliers in the rue de Richelieu in 1782, called *La Grande Taverne de Londres* (modelled on the London Tavern, where Farley was chief chef) and famous for its roast beef and boiled vegetables (see also page 44). There were many establishments where food was cooked to be consumed off the premises. The *rôtisseurs* (roasters), known in the fourteenth century in the rue de la Huchette, were very highly thought of and had a powerful guild which never hesitated to resort to arms to keep their monopoly. *Traiteurs* (from the French, to treat) were places where whole joints, fowls, etc. were cooked, and unless they were also wine-sellers, this food could not be eaten on the premises. Brillat-Savarin, writing about 1770 said: 'strangers had as yet few resources . . . it was possible to go to the *traiteurs*, but they could only sell whole pieces; and he who wished to entertain friends had to order in advance . . . [they] left the great city without knowing the resources and delights of Parisian cuisine.'

In 1765 a soup-seller called Boulanger, in the St Honoré quarter, gave the name 'restaurant' to the world, for above his soup-kitchen he hung a sign, 'Boulanger débite des restaurants divins' (Boulanger sells divine restoratives) which he further embellished in Latin, by 'Venite ad me, vos qui stomacho laboratis; et ego restaurebo vos' or, 'Come unto me, O weary stomachs and I will restore you'. He wanted to extend his menu but because he was not a member of the powerful corporation of *traiteurs*, he was not allowed to sell *ragoûts* or sauces. However, he served a dish of sheep's trotters in white sauce (similiar to Poulette, page 42) and was immediately sued by the *traiteurs*. It became a *cause célèbre*, but Parliament decreed in his favour, and the public hurried to sample his food.

The *table d'hôte* was the forerunner of the restaurant, where everyone sat at the same table, the late-comers at the bottom of the table faring very badly. Foreign visitors sent out for their food and ate it in their rooms at the hostelries. Carving was done at the table, the best parts going to those at the head: it was not until the late eighteenth century that service *à la Russe*, that is, presenting diners with their food already carved, at separate tables, came into being.

The French Revolution saw the abolition of the various food guilds and corporations and many restaurants sprang up, some run by chefs from exiled noble families, allowing everyone, as Brillat-Savarin said: 'to make according to his purse, or according to his appetite, large or delicate meals, which formerly were the perquisite of the very rich'. For information on cafés, see page 42.

Traiteur *and* Marchand de Vin *at the corner of rue des Rondeaux and rue des Prairies, Ménilmontant, c.1852. Photographer, Charles Marville.*

# OMELETTE REINE PÉDAUQUE

## OMELETTE REINE PÉDAUQUE

La Reine Pédauque was a favourite restaurant during the First World War and its tradition continues today in the rue de la Pépinière.

8 eggs
2 tablespoons ground almonds
4 tablespoons cream
2 tablespoons caster (extra-fine) sugar
1 tablespoon butter

½ lb. (2 cups) (227 g.) apple purée
2 tablespoons thick cream
4 tablespoons Kirsch or Calvados
2 stiffly-beaten egg-whites
icing (confectioner's) sugar

Beat the eggs lightly with the ground almonds, caster sugar and 4 tablespoons cream. Heat half the butter so that it is foaming and make one flat omelette with half the egg mixture and put straight away into a buttered ovenproof dish. Then make another omelette with the remaining butter and egg mixture and drain on kitchen paper. Spread the first omelette with the apple purée which has been mixed with the thick cream and 2 tablespoons Kirsch and put the second omelette on top. Cover the whole with the stiffly beaten egg-whites, sprinkle with the icing sugar and put into a very hot oven (425°F.) for about 10 minutes or until the meringue sets and the top is golden.

This makes an excellent and simple sweet as the omelette filling can be made ahead of time, the egg-whites beaten and the whole put into the oven while you are eating the cheese course. Just before serving gently warm the remaining 2 tablespoons of Kirsch in a ladle and when the omelette is on the table pour it over and set fire to it.

Serves 4.

*Posters on wall, Paris, 1917.*

**CASINO DE PARIS**

ORSI

**BOUCOT**

Je laisse tout tomber!
POUR VENIR JOUER
**LA GRANDE REVUE**
DU
**CASINO DE PARIS**

*Gaby Deslys*

Je laisse tout tomber
POUR AMENER
AU
**CASINO DE PARIS**
LES DERNIÈRES NOUVEAUTÉS
d'Angleterre & d'Amérique
DANS
**LA GRANDE REVUE**

*Harry Pilcer*

ORSI

**MAGNARD**

**CASINO DE PARIS**
**GABY DESLYS**
ET
**HARRY PILCER**
DANS
LA GRANDE REVUE DU CASINO DE PARIS
**LAISSE LES TOMBER**
Revue à Grand Spectacle, 2 Actes, 60 Tableaux
de MM. Gustave ARNOULD & Jacques CHARLES
BOUSQUET
★ **BOUCOT** ★
CHRISTIANE Blanche RITTIER LOUVAIN
DERIEUX VANNA · DARTOIS CASSARY
**ROSE-AMY**
La Grande Attraction Américaine
**SHERBO-AMERICAN-BAND**
Mlles MARSAC · Mlle ESSLY Mlle MAURIETTA LHÉRY VELDA · CARLITTA
MAURY BOSKA NONE-HETTE BELLECOURT BERNYS MONTANDON
**LES 48 BEAUTIES GIRLS**
THERVAL · Paul FAIVRE RHEIMS
LEONCE · PRE Fils · GAITO · PAUL JEAN
**PRETTY MYRTILL**
**MAGNARD**
TOUS LES SOIRS à 8h ¼
MATINÉES : JEUDIS DIMANCHES & FETES

# CONSOMMÉ RÉJANE

Réjane was an actress who appeared in many of the successful operettas of Henri Meilhac at the Vaudeville theatre, among them La Belle Hélène, Frou-Frou and Décoré.

Drouant opened in 1880 in the place Gaillon, still flourishes today. It has been in the same family since it was established, and is noted for its excellent fish, shellfish and game dishes. Since 1905 the Académie Goncourt has met there on the first Tuesday of every month to discuss current literature (also to enjoy a roasted lobster perhaps). Annually in November the ten members meet to bestow the Prix Goncourt for the year's best novel. These lunches take place in Salon 15, a private dining-room on the third floor, furnished with Louis XVI chairs.

Many of the classical nineteenth-century French dishes were made to honour celebrities. Réjane had several dishes named for her.

CONSOMMÉ RÉJANE consists of 2 pints (1 l.) white consommé garnished with the breast of chicken, the white part of two leeks and 1 potato, all cut matchstick thin (*julienne*), and poached gently for 10 minutes.

## SAUMON À LA RÉJANE (Salmon cutlets Réjane)

Turbot, halibut, swordfish etc. can also be used.

| | |
|---|---|
| 4 cutlets salmon | salt and freshly ground |
| ½ pint (1 cup) (0.285 l.) white wine | pepper |
| | 6 sprigs watercress |
| 2 sprigs each: chopped parsley and chervil | 4 tablespoons butter |
| | 2 teaspoons flour |

Butter an ovenproof dish, then put the cutlets on top, season, and sprinkle the chopped parsley and chervil on top. Pour the wine around, cover with greased paper or foil and bake in a moderate oven (350°F.) or poach on top of the stove for 20–30 minutes depending on the thickness of the fish. Pour off the liquid into a saucepan and keep the fish warm. Blanch the watercress in boiling salted water for 2 minutes, drain and dry, then either sieve, or chop very finely. Mix the flour with 2 teaspoons butter and add this to the fish stock, bring to the boil, stirring, and cook for 5 minutes until thickened and slightly reduced. Beat the watercress with the remaining butter and add this to the sauce, beating with a wire whisk. Serve over the salmon.

Serves 4.

4    *Gabrielle Réjane (1856–1920), the well-known actress, arriving at Drouant's restaurant, place Gaillon, in her* calèche, *c.1890s. Photographer, Giuseppe Primoli.*

# CHOU ROUGE À LA D'ORLÉANS

*Les Halles from* on alles *(in the twelfth century) is the district where the market, now moved to Rungis, stood until recently, and where all the fresh food that fed Paris was sold. La Corporation des Forts des Halles is the oldest of the Paris corporations and was founded by King (St) Louis in 1250. See also pages 14 and 53.*

## CHOU ROUGE À LA D'ORLÉANS
### (Red Cabbage à la d'Orléans)

This dish came about in the following amusing way. In the reign of Louis XV a market gardener from Orléans brought red cabbage to les Halles market, but on account of its colour nobody would buy it. The gardener, loath to lose the money for his large crop, thought of a means to get the *haut-monde* at least to try it. When Louis XIV's sister-in-law died in 1721 all society went to her mass at Saint-Sulpice where at the door a servant in black handed each lady a sealed envelope, saying: 'Her Royal Highness the Duchesse d'Orléans instructed me, with her last breath, to hand a letter to each of her friends today.' One lady could not resist opening it during the service, and read: 'Tender friend, I cannot render a better and more valuable service than to leave you my favourite recipe on how to use red cabbage in cooking.' The recipe followed and the letter was signed, 'Charlotte Elizabeth of Bavaria, Duchesse d'Orléans'. Each letter read the same, and the King was so amused when the story reached Versailles that he insisted on tasting the recipe. It later became one of Madame de Pompadour's favourite dishes which she often made herself, for the King. The recipe is as follows:

'Cook a medium sized sliced red cabbage in four pints of bouillon with two slices of cooking apple and an onion stuck with clove, and add two glasses of good red wine. Sprinkle generously with spices and let it simmer for several hours.'

*Les Halles market, rue Rambuteau, c.1890s. Photographer, Eugène Atget.*

# CANETON AUX OLIVES

*This humble restaurant on the site of an earlier auberge founded in the sixteenth century, mentioned by Madame de Sévigné in her letters and the setting for part of a Dumas novel, is a long way from the sumptuous setting of the present restaurant which is owned by M. Claude Terrail, the grandson of the owner of the Café Anglais (page 79), although M. Frédéric was the creator of the famous pressed duck flambé which is still the* pièce de résistance *at La Tour d'Argent. He also had the foresight to buy the magnificent wine cellar of the Café Anglais when that establishment closed in 1913. On the ground floor of the present restaurant is an exact replica of the table, with the original silver, crystal and china of the dinner served on 7th June 1867 at the Café Anglais to Czar Alexander II, the Czarevitch, Wilhelm I and Bismarck, (said to have cost 400 francs per head) which was one of the most notable dinners of 'la Belle Epoque'.*

La Tour d'Argent has its own duck farms to supply the many duck recipes on the menu. The following was kindly given by Pierre Descreux, Chef des Cuisines of La Tour d'Argent.

## CANETON AUX OLIVES (Duck with olives)

4 lb. (approx. $1\frac{3}{4}$ kg.) duckling
8 tablespoons olive oil
3 chopped shallots
$\frac{1}{2}$ pint (1 cup) (0.285 l.) dry white wine
salt and freshly ground black pepper

$\frac{3}{4}$ pint ($1\frac{1}{2}$ cups) (0.427 l.) sauce brune (see page 95), or thickened consommé
30 pimento-stuffed olives
4 tablespoons finely chopped pistachio nuts

Season the duck and put into a roasting tin with half the olive oil, then roast in a moderate oven (375°F.) for 1 hour. Cool slightly, then remove the breast, legs and second joints (skin if liked) and keep them hot without further cooking.

Defat and chop up the carcase. Soften the shallots in the remaining olive oil together with the carcase. Drain off the oil and add the white wine. Then reduce this over a hot flame to about half. Add the sauce brune or consommé and cook for a further 20 minutes. Pass through a strainer, then add the olives. Add the duck meat and joints and heat up for a few minutes at a gentle simmer.

Serve the duck on a warmed serving dish with the olives around, pour over the sauce, and sprinkle the pistachio nuts over all.

Serves 4.

*Frédéric Delair, the patron of La Tour d'Argent, Quai de la Tournelle, c.1890.*

# POULE-AU-POT HENRI IV

*The Pont Neuf is the oldest bridge in Paris, built by Androuet du Cerceau between 1578 and 1604 during the reign of Henri IV (a statue of whom now dominates the bridge), the much-loved monarch who said: 'I want there to be no peasant in my kingdom so poor that he is unable to have a chicken in his pot every Sunday.' He loved the Seine and used to immerse the young Dauphin in it. When the bridge was far from complete, he jumped from pier to pier until he had gone the whole length. When told that several of his citizens had drowned while doing this, he replied: 'Ah, yes, but they weren't kings.'*

*'. . . . the beauty of the western prospect which meets the eyes of the passenger over the Pont Neuf . . . and in truth it is a splendid view!' G. W. M. Reynolds, Pickwick Abroad or the Tour in France, 1839.*

## POULE-AU-POT HENRI IV (King Henri IV's Chicken-in-the-Pot)

1 large chicken about 4–5 lb. (2–2¼ kg.) with giblets.

COURT BOUILLON

Gizzard, heart, neck, wingtips etc. of bird
knuckle of veal, if available
3 small carrots
2 small white turnips
3 large onions, 1 stuck with 2 cloves
2 leeks
1 stalk celery
bayleaf, sprig parsley
3 quarts (3.42 l.) water
coarse salt and pepper

STUFFING

5 slices stale crustless white bread
½ cup milk
1 thick slice, chopped ham or bacon
the liver of the bird, chopped
pinch of mace or nutmeg
2 chopped garlic cloves
2 tablespoons chopped parsley
sprig of tarragon or chervil, chopped
2 small eggs or 1 large
salt and pepper

First make the court bouillon by simmering all the ingredients together in a large saucepan for 1 hour after removing any scum which forms. To make the stuffing, soak the bread in the milk and when it is absorbed, mash it up then add all the other ingredients, finely chopped, mixing the eggs in last. Put this into the bird at both ends, and tie or skewer firmly. Let the court bouillon cool and remove any fat, then bring to the boil and lower the chicken into it (if put into muslin it is easier to remove), and simmer very gently for about 1½ hours, then test to see if it is cooked; if not, cook for another ½ hour, but on no account let it overcook. The broth is served separately with a few vegetables, the chicken carved, the stuffing sliced then put on to a warmed serving dish with a little of the broth poured over the top. Freshly cooked vegetables and coarse salt accompany it.

Serves 4–6.

*The Pont-Neuf, La Cité, 1852.*

11

# POT-AU-FEU

*The 'Maquis' was a vast unsalubrious district in Montmartre covered with overgrown vegetation of all kinds, weeds and vivid patches of wild flowers, and with broken-down shacks. It was cleaned up and most of the derelict buildings pulled down about 1904–5. The poet Dalechamps called the shop owner in the photograph, 'Ministre de la Mort'.*

## POT-AU-FEU (Boiled beef with vegetables)

This is two dishes in one, the beef broth or *bouillon* being served first, followed by the beef and vegetables. The meat is called *'le Bouilli'* and from this comes 'bully' beef, so called by Allied soldiers in the First World War.

| | |
|---|---|
| 4 lb. (approx. 2 kg.) lean rump or flank beef, cut in two | 1 trimmed head celery |
| | 6 leeks |
| 1½ lb. (approx. 691 g.) shin beef and bone, cracked | 1 large clove garlic |
| cracked knuckle of veal | bayleaf and bouquet garni of herbs |
| ½ lb. (227 g.) ox liver | 1 tablespoon coarse salt |
| 6 carrots | 8 pints (16 cups) (4.54 l.) water |
| 3 turnips | |
| 1 large onion stuck with 2 cloves | black pepper |

Put the meat (tied up) and bones in a large saucepan (see page 65 for French *marmite*), add the cold water and let it come to the boil gently, and when the scum rises, skim off thoroughly. When the scum turns to a thin white foam it can be left. Add the vegetables, herbs, pepper and salt, cover, but leave a small gap for the steam to escape, and simmer very, very gently for 3 hours, then add the liver and cook for ½ hour. Leave to get cold and take off all fat. Ladle out as much soup as is needed, reheat in another pan, and serve first.

Many of the vegetables will be overcooked so it is advisable to cook fresh vegetables of your choice for serving with the meat. Remove the larger pieces of meat, slice and put on to a warmed dish, surround with fresh, cooked vegetables and pour over a very little of the bouillon. This is eaten with coarse salt; pickled gherkins; horseradish; capers; mustard, or dill pickles, whatever is preferred.

The remaining meat is good minced up and made into croquettes, hashed beef, meatballs, Shepherd's pie and so on. It is also excellent served as:

SALADE PARISIENNE, which is thinly sliced beef layered with sliced, boiled potatoes, each layer being covered with chopped shallots or onion, gherkins, and a lot of chopped parsley all highly seasoned with a dressing of 4 tablespoons olive oil mixed with mustard, capers, and 1 tablespoon wine vinegar.

Serves about 10.

*Junk shop in the 'Maquis', rue Caulaincourt, Montmartre, 1904.*

# CÔTES DE PORC CHARCUTIÈRE

*In 1476 the* charcutiers *were given the monopoly of selling pork, both cooked and raw, but they had to buy the meat from butchers. They mostly sold cooked pork during the fifteenth century and specialized in various sausages. In the sixteenth century they were allowed to kill the pigs, but from 1664 they were not allowed to keep pigs within 21 leagues of Paris. This obtained until an abbatoir was set up in the city. An ancient famous Ham Fair (*Foire aux jambons*) takes place annually in Paris when the stalls are laden with all the magnificent pâtés, sausages, galantines, black puddings (*boudins*), hams and* foie gras *that France has to offer.*

OEUFS À LA CHARCUTIÈRE are fried or poached eggs arranged on a dish alternately with flat cakes of grilled sausagemeat, or sausages, covered with Charcutière sauce as given above.

## CÔTES DE PORC CHARCUTIÈRE
### (Pork chops Charcutière)

4 large pork chops
1 tablespoon oil or lard
 (optional)
salt and pepper

FOR THE SAUCE
1 tablespoon lard or butter
1 medium finely chopped
 onion
½ pint (1 cup) (0.285 l.)
 consommé
6 gherkins cut in thin strips

Heat the oil or lard and brown the chops well on both sides: or if preferred grill them under a medium grill, seasoning to taste. Make the sauce by heating the fat and cooking the onion until it is soft and only slightly coloured. Add the consommé and let it boil for a few minutes, then add the pork chops and simmer, covered, for about 10 minutes, very gently. Just before serving add the gherkins chopped matchstick thin. Another method is to brush the chops with Dijon mustard before adding them to the sauce. Serve with puréed potatoes in the middle of the dish, the chops around, with the sauce poured over.

*At the* charcuterie *stall, Les Halles, le marché de Prouvaires, 1898.*

# BŒUF À LA MODE

Pigeons were first domesticated in the 5th Egyptian dynasty about 3000 B.C.: the pigeon-post system was said to have been established by a Sultan in Baghdad in 1150. The pigeon-post was used extensively by the French in 1848, in 1870 and also during the First World War. Tir aux pigeons (the shooting of semi-tame pigeons, with tail feathers clipped, released from traps) can be traced from 1793, but in the nineteenth century it was a popular social pastime, both in France and in England. However, after a campaign against the cruelty involved, in 1906, clay pigeons were substituted at Hurlingham Club in London, and after a similar outcry made by the London Times in 1921 live pigeon shooting was also discontinued in many parts of France.

## BŒUF À LA MODE (Beef à la Mode)

| | |
|---|---|
| 4 lb. (approx. 2 kg.) lean boneless rump beef | 1 calf's foot, or 2 pig's feet (or aspic powder if above unobtainable) |
| 3 tablespoons oil or dripping | |
| ½ bottle white wine | 1 large sliced onion |
| bouquet of parsley, bayleaf, tarragon | 8 carrots |
| 2 tablespoons brandy | salt and pepper |

This dish must be made the day before it is needed.

Trim the beef of fat or gristle and tie in a round. Heat the oil and brown it all over, lift out and sauté the sliced onion in the fat. Put back the meat, also the calf's foot, split in two, add the herbs, salt and pepper, the wine and enough water to cover the meat. Cover, and simmer on a low flame for 2½ hours. Then add the carrots, scraped, but left whole, and let them cook until tender. Remove the beef and the carrots, strain the stock and let it get cold. When cold remove all fat from the top: carve the beef (trimming off all fat) into thin slices and place in the dish it will be served from. Add the carrots cut into rounds. Heat up the defatted stock, add the brandy and let it boil for 1 minute. Cool slightly, then gently pour over the beef and the carrots and put in a cold place. When cold it will be a thick jelly, and is delicious eaten this way with potatoes baked in their jackets. It can also be eaten hot if liked, but the delicious flavour will be lost.

If using aspic powder, measure the stock after cooking the meat and add 1 level tablespoon per pint (0.57 l.) of boiling liquid, stir until it is quite dissolved before pouring over the meat. Any small flecks of fat should be removed before serving and the whole can be garnished with chopped parsley if liked. It makes an extremely good buffet dish with a green salad.

Serves 8–10.

*At the* Tir aux Pigeons, *Bois de Boulogne, c.1892.*

# SOLE NORMANDE

*One of the most famous early Paris restaurants alas now no more, although L'Escargot-Montorgueil with its panelled dining-room in the same street established in 1830 still continues to delight gastronomes. Au Rocher de Cancale was well known for excellent fish, and at the time when Paris restaurants vied with one another in ways of cooking sole, chef Langlais created Sole Normande there in 1837 to rival Sole Marguery and Sole Dugléré (see page 44).*

*Brillat-Savarin writes in 1825: 'Connoisseurs still remember the names of several artists who have shone in Paris since the invention of the restaurant: names such as Beauvilliers, Méot, Robert, . . . and Baleine (au Rocher de Cancale) . . . to the care he took to have excellent fish.'*

'An adjournment (*sic*) to the Rocher de Cancale – the most celebrated *restaurant* in the world – in the rue Montorgueil, was accordingly effected . . .'
G. W. M Reynolds, *Pickwick Abroad or the Tour in France,* 1839

## SOLE NORMANDE (other thick white fish such as turbot, flounder etc. can be used)

2 sole about 1 lb. (454 g.) each
¼ pint (½ cup) (0.142 l.) fish stock (see below)
1 glass dry white wine or cider

6 button mushrooms
12 mussels or oysters
6 peeled (½ cup) shrimps
2 tablespoons butter
1 tablespoon lemon juice
salt and pepper

FOR THE SAUCE
1 tablespoon butter
1 tablespoon flour
½ pint (1 cup) (0.285 l.) stock from the soles

1 egg yolk
2 tablespoons cream
salt and pepper

Have the fish filleted but keep the skin and bones. Put the bones, skin and trimmings into a saucepan with water to cover, wine and seasoning, and simmer for ½ hour, then strain and reserve the stock. Poach the fillets in this for 5 minutes then remove and put into a well-buttered ovenproof dish. To the stock add the mussels and poach until they open, then lift out and take from the shells: put the shrimps and mushrooms in the stock and lightly poach them for a few minutes, then skim out and put with the mussels around the fish. Pour over the lemon juice and season. Pour a quarter of the strained fish stock around, cover and cook in a moderate oven (350°F.) for 20 minutes. Meanwhile make the sauce, by melting the butter, adding the flour and then the remaining fish stock, stirring all the time until smooth, and season to taste. Mix the cream with the egg-yolk, and off the heat stir into the sauce, reheat, but do not reboil. Pour over the fish and glaze under a hot grill: garnish with croûtons of fried bread.

Serves 4.

*Au Rocher de Cancale, rue Montorgueil, July, 1907.*

# POTAGE AUX LEGUMES

St Vincent de Paul (1576–1660) was at one time the priest of the parishes of Clichy, du Roule, de la Madeleine and d'Antin and established the Oeuvre des Enfants Trouvés, the foundling hospital in Paris. To his Sisters of Charity he gave the following recipe for vegetable soup.

'Fill a large pot with five buckets of water, put into it twenty-five pounds of bread, seven quarters of fat, four pints of peas, white turnips, leeks and onions and salt, for 14 sols. The lot will not cost more than 100 sols for a hundred people.'

## POTAGE AUX LEGUMES (vegetable soup is still popular in Paris)

| | |
|---|---|
| 1 large sliced onion | 3 medium cabbage leaves, diced |
| 2 carrots, diced | |
| 2 small white turnips, diced | 2 stalks celery, diced |
| 2 medium potatoes, diced | sprig of thyme |
| 1 cup peas | 2 tablespoons parsley |
| 2 heaped tablespoons butter | salt and pepper |
| 4 pints (8 cups) (2.28 l.) stock | 2 tablespoons cream |
| 2 leeks, diced | (optional) |

Melt $1\frac{1}{2}$ tablespoons of butter and sauté the onion in it until it is soft, then add all the other vegetables cut into dice. Stir continuously for about 7 minutes while they are cooking. Then add the herbs, finely chopped, and the stock. Let it come to the boil, season, cover and simmer gently for about 1 hour. Put it all through a vegetable mill or liquidizer, taste again for seasoning, and serve hot, either with a knob of butter in each dish or with a little cream.

Serves 6–8

The street soup sellers (Marchands du Soupe) c.1902.

# PAIN DE CAMPAGNE

## PAIN DE CAMPAGNE (French country bread)

1 lb. (4 cups) (454 g. approx.)
   plain bread flour
1 packet (2 teaspoons) dried
   yeast
1 tablespoon sugar
2 teaspoons salt
1 tablespoon lard or
   margarine

¾ pint (1½ cups) (0.427 l.)
   tepid water
1 tablespoon melted butter,
   or egg-white
1 polythene bag large enough
   to take the mixing bowl
*see below

First preheat the oven to 450°F., then in a bowl dissolve the yeast and sugar in the tepid water. (Do not have it more than hand-hot or it will kill the yeast.) Leave for about 10 minutes. Meanwhile rub the fat into the flour and salt, then add the liquid and work to a firm dough until the sides of the bowl are clean. It may need a little more flour, but do not make it dry. Turn on to a lightly floured surface and knead for about 4 minutes until firm and elastic and no longer sticky. Shape into a ball, put back into the mixing bowl and put the lot into the polythene bag, tied loosely. Leave until the dough is double in size (about 1 hour). Turn out on to a lightly floured surface and without working the dough too much divide into 2 parts, grease a baking sheet, and shape dough into long, chubby shapes. Mark a row of diagonal slits across the tops with a sharp knife, cover and leave in a warm place for about 15 minutes. Brush with the butter or egg-white to glaze and bake for 5 minutes at 450°F., then lower the oven to 375°F. for 40–45 minutes. The loaves will sound hollow when tapped on the bottom if cooked.

This dough can also be made into rolls if preferred, in which case they will only need about 25 minutes cooking time.

*To ensure a crisp yet tender crust put a flat pan of boiling water on the lowest rack of the oven during cooking.

22   *Workmen resting on the grass, Longchamps, Bois de Boulogne; the farm of Longchamps having been pulled down to make first, a review ground, and later the racecourse, 1857 (see also page 60).*

# NOISETTES D'AGNEAU RIVOLI

The western end of the rue de Rivoli has one of the most beautiful shopping arcades in Europe and the shops sell articles worthy of the situation. The bookshop where Thackeray browsed is still there, as is the Hotel Meurice so beloved of English and American visitors in the last century. The arcades were designed and executed by Charles Percier and Pierre Fontaine in 1811 under the aegis of Napoleon I and named by him after a town in Italy where he vanquished the Austrians in 1797.

'. . . conducted him up the Rue de Rivoli . . . The young Englishman was astonished at the splendour of the street, and stood for a long time to admire the mighty piles of the palace of the Tuileries with its beautiful gardens on one side, and the uniform range of the lofty houses upon the other.'
G. W. M. Reynolds, *Pickwick Abroad or the Tour in France*, 1839.

## NOISETTES D'AGNEAU RIVOLI
(*Noisettes* are the 'eye' of a thick rib or loin cutlets: when trimmed into rounds they resemble a small fillet)

12 noisettes of lamb
2 tablespoons oil or butter
salt and freshly ground
  pepper
1 glass Madeira wine
4–6 tablespoons consommé
24 button mushrooms

Heat the oil or butter in a heavy *cocotte* pot and sauté the noisettes on all sides according to taste. If liked underdone then about 7 minutes in all should suffice. Remove to a warmed serving dish and keep warm. Pour off any excess fat and scrape down the sides of the pan, then add the Madeira and stir well. Let it reduce for a minute over a hot flame, then add the consommé and the small mushrooms. Simmer very gently for about 7 minutes and season to taste. The mushrooms should be soft, but still firm.

Serve the sauce over the noisettes, or if preferred, the noisettes can be put back into the sauce and the whole dish can be served from the *cocotte*. This dish is accompanied by Pommes de Terre Anna (page 79).

Serves 4–6 depending on the size of the noisettes.

*Shopping arcades in the rue de Rivoli, c.1880s.*

# GNOCCHI À LA PARISIENNE

*For many years the rue de la Paix has been well known for its jewellery shops and* bijouterie *(Cartier is at number 13), and it was a favourite shopping place for both the* haut monde *and the* demi-monde. *After an evening at the Opera they frequented nearby cafés such as Café de la Paix (see page 33), the Café de Paris or the Café Riche, of which the Goncourt brothers wrote in their journal for October 1857: 'The Café Riche seems to be in a fair way to become a camping ground of literary people who wear gloves . . .' It was at the Café Hardy (boulevard des Italiens) in 1804 that the first fork luncheon (*déjeuner à la fourchette*) was given. The beautiful little Théâtre Royal l'Italien with its spheroidal interior was in a nearby square, and this prompted Parisian chefs to make their own version of Italian gnocchi.*

## GNOCCHI À LA PARISIENNE

Made from choux paste (*pâte à choux*) invented by the famous chef Carême (one of twenty-five brothers and sisters), who was taken in when a boy, out of charity, by a pastry-cook. He often said that his greatest pleasure was to watch little street urchins devouring pastry made from his recipes.

| | |
|---|---|
| 2 heaped tablespoons butter | 3 tablespoons grated |
| ½ pint (1 cup) (0.285 l.) water | Parmesan cheese* |
| pinch of salt | 4 oz. (1 cup) (113 g.) sifted |
| 4 eggs | flour |
| | a pinch of nutmeg |

*Angle of the avenue de l'Opéra and the rue de la Paix, c.1890s.*

Put the water, butter, salt and nutmeg into a medium saucepan and bring to the boil slowly until the butter has melted. Remove from the heat and add all the sifted flour at once, beating vigorously with a wooden spoon until the dough is smooth and dry. Return to the heat and beat for 1 or 2 minutes until the panada leaves the sides of the pan. Do not overcook or it will get oily. Take off the heat and add an egg in the middle and beat until it is absorbed. Do this each time until all the eggs are taken up, but do not overbeat. Well mix in the cheese until the paste is quite smooth. Leave until cool, then shape into small balls with 2 teaspoons dipped in hot water. (At this point they can be left in a cool place, or deep-frozen for later use.) Heat a large saucepan of salted water and poach the dumplings for about 15 minutes (for sweet buns or canapés bake in a hot oven (425°F.) for about the same time and when risen and golden take them out and slit the side open to release steam) then remove with a slotted spoon, drain and arrange in a buttered baking dish. To serve, either cover with dots of butter and grated Parmesan cheese and heat in a hot oven until golden, or cover with a cream sauce made from heating 1 tablespoon butter, adding 1 tablespoon flour and ½ pint (1 cup) (0.285 l.) warm milk and cream, mixed. Stir until smooth then pour over the top, sprinkle with a little grated Parmesan and bake as above. Serves 4.

*This choux pastry can be used for profiterolles, sweet buns, éclairs, etc. with the addition of 2 teaspoons sugar instead of the cheese.

# SOUPE À L'OIGNON GRATINÉE

*Until a few years ago before les Halles, called the Belly of Paris, moved out to Rungis, many of the market cafés (which have been famous since the Middle Ages for good, cheap food) were open all night for the market workers, one of the specialities being a vast bowl of hot onion soup with a thick crust of bubbling cheese, often followed by a prime cut of beef or pig's trotters. These cafés became a popular rendezvous for visitors as well as Parisians. See also pages 6, 14 and 53.*

## SOUPE À L'OIGNON GRATINÉE
### (Onion soup with cheese)

1½ lb. (681 g.) peeled, sliced onions

2 tablespoons butter and 2 of oil

a pinch of sugar

3½ pints (7 cups) (2 l.) strong beef stock, consommé or bouillon

2 level tablespoons flour

6 heaped tablespoons grated Gruyère, or half each Parmesan and Gruyère cheese

¼ pint (½ cup) (0.142 l.) red wine

3 tablespoons brandy (optional)

salt and freshly ground pepper

6 rounds of 1-inch French bread, dried out in a 300°F. oven for ½ hour, or toasted

Heat the butter and oil in a large saucepan and when hot add the thinly sliced onions. Cook over a low flame turning from time to time until they are soft, then add the salt and sugar. Continue cooking until the onions are an even golden brown. Sprinkle over the flour, add the stock and red wine and stir until it comes to the boil. Lower the heat, cover and simmer very gently for about 1 hour. Taste for seasoning and leave until ready to serve, removing any fat when cold. Meanwhile dry out the bread and grate the cheese. Heat the soup to simmering point, add the brandy if using, and pour into ovenproof individual dishes or one large one, float the bread slices on top and add the cheese to each slice. Either put into a preheated, hot (450°F.) oven or under the grill until the top is bubbling and lightly browned.

Serves 6.

## SOUPE À L'OIGNON SOUFFLÉ

A complete light meal with fruit or a salad. Make the soup as above, add the bread slices, then top with the following soufflé mixture and bake in a preheated oven (450°F.) for 8–10 minutes, or until risen and golden. Serve at once.

2 heaped tablespoons butter

2 heaped tablespoons flour

¾ pint (1½ cups) (0.427 l.) warm milk

6 tablespoons grated cheese as above

2 stiffly-beaten egg-whites

salt and pepper

Heat the butter, stir in the flour letting it cook for 2 minutes, then add the warm milk, stirring until smooth. Add the cheese, let it cool then season and add the beaten egg-whites, folding them in well. Spoon this over the bread and bake as given above.

*'La Belle de Nuit' : the early hours in a café, Les Halles market, rue Rambuteau, 1903.*

# CERVELLES AU BEURRE NOIR

France was one of the first countries in the world to introduce, in the 1870s, big department stores such as the Samaritaine, the Louvre, Bon Marché and Pygmalion to the public. This new development was much praised by Zola in Au Bonheur des Dames. It made an enormous difference, for previously the well-to-do patronized small individual couturiers, modistes and so on. These large stores treated their staff very well, often providing board and lodging, a fortnight's holiday (in 1900) and all fête days free.

'The amount of good that such institutions as these do in France is almost incredible. They are great levellers; they make luxury possible to the poor . . . think what a pleasure it must be to a woman who has never before been within arm's length of such treasures, to hold, to try on, the finest and daintiest of clothes! To the Parisian woman the *Magasin de Louvre,* with its brilliant placards, and bargain days, is much more important than the great palace of the Louvre.'

Dorothy Menpes, *Paris,* 1909.

## CERVELLES AU BEURRE NOIR
### (Brains with black butter)

Black butter is a good and simple sauce for serving over poached white fish, over poached or baked eggs, and sweetbreads.

| | |
|---|---|
| 4 sets calf's brains | a little flour |
| squeeze of lemon juice or wine vinegar | 6 tablespoons butter |
| | 1 tablespoon wine vinegar |
| salt and pepper | 2 tablespoons capers |
| parsley | |

Soak the brains in cold salted water with a squeeze of lemon juice for about an hour. Drain, and remove as much of the membrane as possible without tearing the flesh. Wash and drain, then put into a saucepan, well covering them with cold water, and simmer very gently for about 15 minutes. Drain again and plunge into iced water until cooled. (This preparation should also be done with sweetbreads.) Take out of the water and pat them dry and remove all skin or membrane. Dip them lightly in seasoned flour, then heat 2 tablespoons butter and fry them on all sides until lightly browned, and remove to a warmed serving dish. Remove any pieces from the fat in the pan, then add the remaining butter, heat until it takes on a nut-brown colour, add the vinegar and let it foam. Finally add the capers and serve the sauce poured over the brains, garnished with parsley.

Serves 4.

*Pygmalion department store, rue de Rivoli, c.1900.*

31

# CHOU FARCI

About 1840 literary men, artists and the rich bourgeoisie frequented a café at 10 du boulevard des Capucines called La Grange-aux-Belles, where guitar concerts were held. These were also attended by Philippe-Egalité, who had a private salon there. This went on until the Café de la Paix was built on the same site in the 1870s. Its proximity to the new Opera House which opened in 1875 made it the rendezvous for intellectuals such as Maupassant, Zola, Massenet and, later on, Gide, Valéry and Louÿs, as well as the numerous demi-monde with their sumptuous equipages, furs and jewels. New and elaborate dishes were invented for the clientèle. Consommé du Capucine, a chicken soup garnished with shredded spinach and lettuce chiffonade, with profiterolles (see page 27) filled with chicken purée; and Capucine garnish for meats, of stuffed cabbage leaves, stuffed mushrooms, masked with Sauce Madère, which today would be considered a meal on its own. . . . .

## CHOU FARCI (Stuffed Cabbage)

12 large crisp cabbage leaves
1 large finely chopped onion
1 lb. (454 g.) sausagemeat or
   equivalent minced meat
bouquet of chopped herbs
grated peel and juice of $\frac{1}{2}$
   lemon
1 beaten egg
3 heaped tablespoons fresh
   breadcrumbs
salt and freshly ground
   pepper
a pinch of nutmeg
$1\frac{1}{2}$ pints (3 cups) (0.85 l.)
   stock
3 tablespoons oil

See that the cabbage leaves are unspecked and freshened in cold water before using. Blanch them (or steam) in boiling salted water for 3 minutes, drain carefully and pat dry. Heat the oil and lightly sauté the onion, then mix it into the other ingredients except the stock, leaving the egg until last. Spread a little of this mixture on each leaf, roll up and either tie with twine or secure with a skewer. Heat up the oil the onion was sautéed in and lightly fry the cabbage rolls, transferring them at once to an ovenproof dish. Pour the seasoned stock around, cover and cook in a moderate oven (350°F.) for about 1 hour.

Choose large mushrooms for stuffing, put them in a lightly greased dish and spoon over a tablespoon of cooked rice mixed with chopped herbs. Put a knob of butter on top and bake in a hot oven (400°F.) for about 20 minutes.

A Madeira flavoured sauce can be simply made by draining off the cabbage liquid into a small saucepan and adding 3 tablespoons of Madeira. Boil gently to reduce a little, then thicken by adding a *beurre manié* of 1 tablespoon butter worked with 2 heaped teaspoons of flour. Stir until the sauce is smooth. Serves 4–6.

*Evening on the boulevard des Capucines, c.1850.*

# GIGOT OU ÉPAULE D'AGNEAU BRAISÉ AUX HARICOTS

*The École Polytechnique, a military school of higher education, was founded in 1794 and to this day supplies many of the civil and military engineers employed in the French civil service, army, navy and air force.*

## GIGOT OU ÉPAULE D'AGNEAU BRAISÉ AUX HARICOTS (Braised leg or shoulder of lamb with haricot beans)

| | |
|---|---|
| 5 lb. (2¼ kg.) leg or shoulder lamb or mutton | ¼ pint (½ cup) (0.142 l.) red wine |
| 4 tablespoons lard or oil | 3 sprigs parsley |
| 2 sliced carrots | salt and pepper |
| 2 large sliced onions | 1 lb. (454 g.) dried haricot beans soaked overnight* |
| 1 bayleaf | |
| ½ teaspoon rosemary or thyme | 2½ pints (5 cups) (1½ l.) boiling salted water |
| 2 garlic cloves | |
| 1½ pints (3 cups) (0.85 l.) stock | bouquet of herbs |
| | pepper |

*Preliminary cooking may be done in a pressure cooker; time needed is 20 minutes after pressure is reached.

It is essential to have a heavy ovenproof casserole large enough to hold all the ingredients including the beans. Heat the lard or oil and brown the meat all over, then take it out and lightly soften the vegetables in the oil. Pour off most of the oil but leave any pan juices and to them add the wine, scraping down the sides so that it amalgamates. Put back the meat, fatty side up, add the vegetables, herbs, and enough stock to come to three-quarters of the way up. Season, then cover and cook in a moderate oven (350°F.) for 40 minutes to the pound for well-done meat, and 30 minutes for medium. Turn at least once during cooking time. Meanwhile drain the soaked beans and put them in a pan with the boiling water, herbs and pepper and simmer for 1–1½ hours, or pressure cook as above (if using a pressure cooker use only half the water). They should have absorbed almost all the liquid and still be a little hard. Lift the meat out of the juices a half hour before it is ready, take off as much fat from the stock as possible and taste for seasoning. Add the meat and put the beans around. Bring to boiling point on top of the stove and put back in the oven until the beans are ready and the meat tender, about ½ hour, but this depends on the meat and beans used. The meat can be cooked ahead of time and degreased if liked, then the beans half-cooked and added, as above. Lentils can be used instead of beans if preferred.

Serves about 10.

THE PRESSURE COOKER was first invented in 1679 by the French physicist Denis Papin in London, where he worked closely with the Irish scientist, Robert Boyle. He died in obscurity and penury in 1712. Perhaps one day the pressure cooker will be known as a 'Papineur', for then justice would be done.

*Playing billiards, École Polytechnique, rue Cardinal Lemoine, c.1860s.*

# ESCOFFIER'S SAUCE DIABLE

*The Moulin Rouge, as well as providing superb entertainment with such artistes as Yvette Guilbert and La Goulue (page 38), was also renowned for its restaurant, which was frequented by all the well-known writers and painters of the period, especially Toulouse Lautrec, Gustave Doré, the Goncourt brothers and their circle: Émile Zola and Alphonse Daudet would talk of the hardship of their early days. Zola recalled times when he pawned his coat and trousers and had to stay home in his shirt. Escoffier, the famous chef, started his career at the Moulin Rouge, and went on to the Savoy and Carlton Hotels in London. This restaurant closed about 1883: today the character is very changed.*

*Prostitutes have had an up and down time in Paris, since King St Louis forbad them to dress like decent women, his wife Marguerite de Provence having given the kiss of peace at a Mass to a well-dressed woman standing next to her, whom she discovered was a harlot. Up until 1914 no prostitute was allowed to solicit unless she wore a hat, or open a brothel without the Prefect's permission.*

*About 1840 'Lorettes' appeared (so called because their favourite district was Notre-Dame-de-Lorette), recruited from abandoned wives and tradesmen's daughters, who did not solicit, but never refused presents of any kind. In 1844 the painter Eugène Delacroix wrote to George Sand: 'This new district has arisen to make ardent men like me dizzy . . . the first object that struck the eyes of my virtue was a magnificent lorette dressed in black satin and velvet, who, getting out of a cabriolet, with the unconcern of a goddess let me see her leg up to her navel . . .'*

## ESCOFFIER'S SAUCE DIABLE (Devil sauce for serving with grilled poultry, pigeons, or for reheating slices of cooked meat or ham)

For other Escoffier recipes see page 41.

| | |
|---|---|
| 6 finely sliced shallots | 2 cups (1 pint) (0.57 l.) |
| $\frac{1}{2}$ pint (1 cup) (0.285 l.) | consommé |
| white wine | 2 tablespoons butter |
| $\frac{1}{2}$ teaspoon cayenne pepper | |

Put the shallots into a pan with the wine and boil rapidly until it is reduced to two-thirds, then add the consommé and reduce again to the same amount. Season with the pepper, strain, and before serving add the softened butter in small pieces.

SALADE LORETTE is Corn Salad (*Mâche* in French) mixed with thin slices of cooked beet and sliced celery covered with a dressing in the proportion of 4 tablespoons olive oil to one of wine vinegar, seasoned to taste.

*Ladies of the town at the Moulin Rouge, Montmartre, c.1880.*

# LE VOLCAN AUX MARRONS

L

La Goulue (second from left) was a much loved entertainer, the toast of Paris, immortalized by Toulouse Lautrec (1864–1901) in his paintings and posters. Born Louise Weber, her warm personality completely captured her audience. She died in poverty in Montmartre in 1929, looked after by her neighbours. Valentin le-Désossé, known as 'Don Quixote of the dance', with his melancholy expression was the perfect foil for her.

Edmond Heuzé wrote this of La Goulue: 'La Goulue était une fille essentiellement peuple, une fille du trottoir. C'était un être tout à fait special. Il faut l'avoir vue danser, ne fut-ce qu'une fois, pour être confirmé dans cette opinion.' Du Moulin Rouge à l'Institut.

## LE VOLCAN AUX MARRONS
### (Chestnut Volcano)

| | |
|---|---|
| 1 lb. (500 g.) tin sweet chestnut purée | 4½ oz. (1 cup + 1 tablespoon) (125 g.) butter |
| ⅞ pint (½ l.) (1⅜ cups) milk | 3 tablespoons seedless raisins |
| 3 large eggs, separated | 2 measures (jiggers) rum |
| 2 tablespoons rum | |

Separate the eggs, and when breaking them see that one shell is broken cleanly without jagged eges. Reserve the larger part of this shell. Soften the butter (but do not let it boil); then lightly beat the egg-yolks. Mix the milk well into the chestnut purée, then add the beaten egg-yolks, softened butter, raisins and 2 tablespoons rum. Butter a 1½ pint (1 l.) soufflé dish, then beat the egg-whites until stiff, preheat the oven to 425°F., and fold the egg-whites into the chestnut mixture. Keep the larger half of the smooth eggshell nearby. Put the soufflé mixture into the dish, then gently press the eggshell half, open side up, into the centre until it is three parts submerged. Put the dish in the centre of the hot oven for 35 minutes. Meanwhile warm, but on no account boil, the remaining rum, and when the soufflé is ready and on the table, pour the warm rum into the eggshell and set light to it. Serve while it is still burning and take care not to split the eggshell. When several portions have been served gently turn the eggshell upside down and remove. Any rum left inside will mix with the soft centre. Let the guests wait for the soufflé, not the other way round. If put in the oven immediately after the meat course is served, it will cook while the cheese is being eaten.

Serves 4–6.

*La Goulue, Grille d'Egout, Valentin le-Désossé and a friend doing the Can-Can at the Moulin Rouge, c.1880s.*

Café
Bière
AUX PINSONS de BAGNOLET
VINS
BALANÇOIRES
& JEUX DIVERS
TERRAIN A LOUER
S'ADRESSER ICI
103

# TRUITE À LA MEUNIÈRE

Guinguettes *were open-air taverns with gardens where one could dance, drink, eat and play various games, so called after M. Guinget who started them in the 1670s at Ménilmontant.*

'I indulged in a cheap idyll the other day . . . dining at what is called in Parisian parlance a *guinguette*. . . . It was a very humble style of entertainment, but the most frantic pursuit of pleasure can do no more than succeed, and this was a success. Your table is spread under a trellis which scratches your head – spread chiefly with fried fish – and an old man who looks like a very high-toned political exile comes and stands before it and sings a doleful ditty on the respect due to white hairs. You testify by the bestowal of a couple of coppers . . . and he is speedily replaced by a lad with one arm, who treats you to something livelier: "A la bonne heure; parlez-moi de ça!"'
Henry James, *Parisian Sketches*, August 1876.

## TRUITE À LA MEUNIÈRE (also for sole, plaice, flounder etc.)

| | |
|---|---|
| 4 large trout | 1 large lemon |
| 6 tablespoons butter | 2 teaspoons chopped parsley |
| a little flour, seasoned | salt and freshly ground pepper |

Clean the fish and leave them whole, then roll them in seasoned flour. Heat 3 tablespoons butter until foaming but not brown, and cook the fish slowly on each side on a low heat for 5 minutes so that it has time to cook through without burning. Raise the heat just before they are ready, to brown them. In all it should take about 10 minutes. Put on to a warmed serving dish and sprinkle with juice of half the lemon and a little chopped parsley. Keep warm. Add the remaining butter to the pan juices and heat until dark gold, then pour over the hot fish and serve with lemon slices rolled in parsley. If liked about 4 tablespoons halved, blanched almonds can be added to the last butter, browned slightly and poured over the fish.

Serves 4.

## SOLE LUTÈCE (a recipe of M. Escoffier, *c.*1900)

Lutetia was the Roman name for the Île de la Cité, which had been settled by a Celtic tribe called the Parisii, who were displaced by the Romans in 52 B.C.

Cook 8 sole fillets as above, then lay them on a bed of shredded spinach tossed in butter. On top put $\frac{1}{2}$ grated onion and 4 sliced artichoke bottoms, both sautéed lightly in butter. Put a border of freshly sautéed potatoes around and pour over the lightly browned hot butter just before serving.

*Wine, seesaws and games at Pinson's Guinguette, Porte de Ménilmontant, c.1880s.*

# SAUCE POULETTE

Originally cafés sold only coffee, brought to France first in 1669 by Sulieman Aga, although it was known in London in 1652 where immediately many coffee-shops sprang up. An Armenian called Pascal opened a coffee-shop at the Easter St-Germain Fair (first recorded in the twelfth century) in 1699, but when he moved to the Quai de l'École his trade fell off. In 1686 a Sicilian called Procopio dei Coltelli opened the first café in the world in the rue de l'Ancienne Comédie, where it still stands although it is now a restaurant. Molière, Voltaire, La Fontaine, D'Alambert, Diderot and many other brilliant men went there. The widow Fournier was the first to supply newspapers; the Café des Grâces (rue l'Arbre-sec) the first to have billiards and the Café de la Régence (near Palais-Royal) became famous for its chess-players. Originally cakes and ices were sold, but by the late eighteenth century soups, eggs and chicken dishes were the customary fare. See Poule-au-pot page 11.

Early in the nineteenth century the fashionable café was Tortoni's: '. . . this establishment was so much in vogue that it was difficult to get an ice there; after the opera and theatres were over, the boulevards were literally choked up with the carriages of the great people of the court and the Faubourg St-Germain bringing their guests to Tortoni's.' Reminiscences and Reflections of Captain Gronow, 1862.

Gas lighting increased the number of cafés and by 1890 respectable women and their families frequented them. See also pages 27 and 33.

## SAUCE POULETTE

An indispensable French sauce for serving with boiled poultry, fish, brains, sweetbreads, frogs legs, mussels, mushrooms or sheep's trotters.

| | |
|---|---|
| 1 pint (2 cups) (0.57 l.) stock or liquid from whatever is being served | 1 lemon |
| | 6 tablespoons cream |
| | 3 egg-yolks |
| 2 heaped tablespoons butter | 1 tablespoon cornflour (cornstarch) |
| 4 oz. (113 g.) mushrooms (omit if serving with mushrooms and use 2 shallots) | 2 sprigs parsley, chopped |
| | salt and pepper |

Slice the mushrooms and cook them lightly in the butter with a squeeze of lemon juice. Bring the stock to the boil, and thicken with the cornflour previously mixed with a little cold stock, stirring until smooth. Reduce heat and simmer. Mix the egg-yolks, cream, lemon juice, parsley and mushrooms and add to the sauce, stirring constantly, to just under boiling point. It will keep in double boiler over hot, but not boiling water, for about ½ hour. Makes 3 cups. It freezes well and can be heated in a *bain-marie*.

*Café Procope, first café in the world, rue de l'Ancienne Comédie (formerly rue des Fossés Saint-Germain), c.1900.*

# SOLE DUGLÉRÉ

The Avenue de l'Opéra was started by Georges Haussmann in 1854 and finished in 1878, the difficulty being the hillock St Roch which raised the elevation of the rue Thérèse and the rue des Pyramides.

*The first restaurant in Paris was opened by Beauvilliers in 1782, followed by 'Aux Trois Frères Provençaux' in the arcade of the Palais-Royal in 1786. It was at this latter restaurant that the chefs Dugléré and Moisson started (see page 19). The arcades and shops around the Palais-Royal were built by Philippe-Egalité, finished in 1784 and rented by him. His relative, Louis XVI, remarked: 'now that you're going to open a shop cousin, we doubtless will only see you on Sunday'. These shops, as in the rue de Rivoli arcade, became the haunt of prostitutes from the late afternoon. Balzac in* Les Illusions Perdues *writes: '. . . le Palais, par excellence, mot qui signifiait alors le temple de la Prostitution.'*

'. . . that mart in the vicinity of a palace – that palace overlooking shops – that unique lounge which has no rival in the world!' G. W. M. Reynolds, *Pickwick Abroad or the Tour in France*, 1839.

## SOLE DUGLÉRÉ

Put 8 sole fillets into a buttered dish with 1 medium finely chopped onion, $\frac{1}{2}$ lb. (227 g.) peeled and chopped tomatoes, a sprinkle of parsley, salt and pepper and $\frac{1}{4}$ pint ($\frac{1}{2}$ cup) (0.142 l.) white wine. Poach gently for 10 minutes, then lift the sole on to a warmed serving dish. Reduce the fish stock, add a *beurre manié* (2 teaspoons butter rolled in flour), the juice of half a lemon and 2 tablespoons of cream. Pour over the fish and brown under the grill.

## ŒUFS OPÉRA (fried eggs with chicken livers and asparagus)

| | |
|---|---|
| 8 eggs | salt and freshly ground pepper |
| 1 lb. (454 g.) chicken livers | 2 tablespoons Madeira wine, |
| 3 tablespoons butter or oil | or sweet, dark vermouth |
| 1 cup consommé | 12 cooked asparagus tips |

Heat 2 tablespoons of butter or oil and fry the chicken livers until pink but not brown inside. Season to taste. Pour off the fat, add the wine, reduce and keep warm. Heat the remaining butter and gently fry the eggs, transferring them to a warm dish. Heat the cooked asparagus in the consommé, lift out and place the livers at one side of the eggs and the asparagus at the other. Reduce the consommé and pour around.

Serves 4.

*Avenue de l'Opéra, near to the Théâtre Français and the Palais-Royal (right of photograph), 1888.*

# P AIN D'ÉPICE

'. . . when the Champs Élysées re-echo to the music of Franconi, or of the various surrounding guinguettes – when the fume of cigar mingles with the fragrance of sweet flowers – when every heart is light . . .' G. W. M. Reynolds, *Pickwick Abroad or the Tour in France*, 1839.

*Ledoyen, the famous restaurant which opened during the Second Empire in the Carré des Champs Élysées, and was built on the site of a simple* guinguette *(see page 41), still flourishes in one of the most beautiful situations in Paris. A speciality in the restaurant is Sole soufflée Ledoyen; there is also an outdoor terrace where drinks are served in sylvan surroundings.*
'. . . all the gingerbread stalls down the Champs Élysées . . .' W. M. Thackeray, 14th July, *Paris Sketch Book*, 1840.

## PAIN D'ÉPICE

(French spice cake, which is what Thackeray calls 'gingerbread'. It keeps well if airtight and should be served thinly sliced, with or without butter, with tea or coffee.)

$\frac{3}{4}$ pint (1$\frac{1}{2}$ cups) (0.427 l.) boiling water
1 level teaspoon anise seeds
$\frac{1}{2}$ lb. (1 cup) (227 g.) liquid honey
10 oz. (1$\frac{1}{4}$ cups) (284 g.) sugar
1 level teaspoon bicarbonate soda

1$\frac{1}{2}$ lb. (6 cups) (681 g.) plain flour
4 tablespoons chopped mixed candied orange and lemon peel
$\frac{1}{2}$ teaspoon each of cinnamon and nutmeg
pinch of salt

First preheat the oven to 350°F., and grease 1 large or 2 small loaf tins. Boil the water with the anise seeds. Add the honey and sugar and stir until both are dissolved. Take off the heat and add the bicarbonate of soda. In a large bowl, mix together the flour, spices, salt and candied peel, then add the strained liquid, stirring all the time. Beat until the mixture is smooth. Pour into the greased tins and bake for 1 hour before testing with a warmed skewer. If it comes out clean then the cake is cooked. If using 2 smaller tins then make the test after 45 minutes.

*A summer afternoon on the Champs Élysées, c.1866.*

CARNAVALET

# VOL-AU-VENT À LA FINANCIÈRE

'. . . and continued his way till he arrived in the Place de la Bourse, where he halted for a moment to admire the splendid building which forms the Exchange of Paris.' G. W. M. Reynolds, *Pickwick Abroad or the Tour in France*, 1839.

## VOL-AU-VENT À LA FINANCIÈRE

'This entrée is pretty and good without a doubt . . . but to cook it perfectly demands the utmost care. This is the essential part of the operation, so that the flakiness of the pastry is not lost in dampness.' Antonin Carême 1784–1833.

PUFF PASTRY
(Pâte Feuilletée)
1 lb. (4 cups) (454 g.)
   plain flour
1 lb. (2 cups) (454 g.) butter
squeeze lemon juice
pinch of salt
6 tablespoons (approx.)
   iced water
egg to glaze

FOR THE FILLING
1 lb. (454 g.) sweetbreads
   (or cooked chicken)
2 slices shredded cooked ham
6 medium chopped
   mushrooms
½ pint (1 cup) (0.285 l.)
   chicken stock
4 tablespoons dry Madeira
   wine
bayleaf, sprig thyme
1 tablespoon arrowroot
salt and pepper

First make the pastry by sieving the flour into a bowl with the salt and a squeeze of lemon juice. Rub 2 tablespoons butter into the flour and add just enough iced water to make a firm dough. Turn on to a floured board and roll to a rectangle about ½-inch thick. Put the whole of the soft remaining butter

*Place de la Bourse, c.1888.*

in the middle, fold over, press the edges well and leave to stand for 15 minutes. With the sealed edges away from you roll the pastry outwards until it is three times the size. Then fold into three, envelope style, turn the open edge to face you and roll again. Leave as before, repeat the folding, rolling and resting so that in all the pastry has been rolled and rested six times. If it still looks fat-streaked give it an extra turn. Wrap and chill before use.

When needed, put on to a floured board and using half the pastry, roll to ¼-inch thick and using an 8-inch oval or round dish as pattern, cut around it and place on a buttered sheet. Repeat this, brushing the bottom layer with cold water before putting the second piece on top and pressing the edges slightly. Cut a circle or oval about 4 inches wide on top to reach the first layer, brush with beaten egg on top and bake in a hot oven (450°F.) for 7 minutes, then reduce to 375°F, for 25–30 minutes more. When cool remove the small 'lid' and scoop out the centre. Put in the filling just before it is needed for reheating.

Prepare the sweetbreads as for the brains on page 31. Chop and add to the sauce, made as follows. Simmer together the chopped ham, herbs, mushrooms and Madeira for ½ hour. Then add the chicken stock, salt and pepper and simmer until slightly reduced. Mix the arrowroot with 2 tablespoons water, mix well into the sauce and stir until smooth. Pour in the pastry case and heat gently for 20 minutes.

Serves 4.

49

# COQ AU VIN

*La Mère Catherine at the top of Montmartre has been a famous inn since 1793 when it was a meeting place for huntsmen ('Le Clairon des Chasseurs'), and is very little changed today. During the French Revolution it was patronized by Danton and other revolutionary figures. The artist Francique Poulbot's house at number 3 is now the Town Hall. La Mère Catherine still caters for local characters as well as tourists, at moderate prices. During the winter months a band plays in the back room on festive occasions. Chicken has always been a speciality of the house.*

See also page 95.

## COQ AU VIN (Chicken in wine)

This recipe can also be used for stewing beef.

3½ lb. (1½ kg.) chicken, jointed
4 oz. (133 g.) diced unsmoked
  bacon
3 tablespoons olive oil
2 tablespoons butter
10 small onions
4 oz. (113 g.) small
  mushrooms

4 tablespoons warmed brandy
1 bottle Beaujolais
1 lump sugar
1 bouquet parsley stalks
  tied together
1 tablespoon chopped parsley
1 heaped tablespoon flour
salt and pepper

1 bayleaf
1 sprig thyme
2 cloves garlic

4 slices bread fried in butter
  as garnish

Heat the olive oil and 2 tablespoons of butter in a heavy casserole, add the diced bacon, and when it turns pale brown add the garlic and onions and sauté for 2 minutes, then add the mushrooms. Remove from pan and keep warm. In the same pan sauté the chicken pieces on both sides, removing to the bacon dish until the whole bird has been lightly browned. Put it all back into the casserole, add salt, pepper, herbs and the juices, then pour the brandy over and set it alight. Shake the flour over the top and turn the joints over, then add the wine and sugar. Bring to boiling point, cover tightly and cook in a moderate oven (350°F.) for ½ hour, then lower the heat to 250°F. and let it cook gently for about 1–1½ hours or until the chicken is tender. Stir once during that time and check that the liquid is not running low, if so add a little more wine. Just before it is ready fork out the parsley bouquet; fry the bread in butter and cut into triangles for the garnish, and keep hot. If the sauce is too thin for your liking, then pour it off and thicken with a *beurre manié*, a knob of butter rolled with flour, stirring briskly until it is well-blended. The sauce should not be too thick as the flour destroys the flavour of the wine. Serve with the croûtons, a good sprinkling of chopped parsley and plain boiled or steamed potatoes (*pommes de terre à l'Anglaise*).

Serves 4–6.

*La Mère Catherine, place du Tertre, Montmartre, c.1900.*

# SOLE À LA BONNE FEMME

The women fish-sellers and other vendors at Les Halles (see also pages 6 and 14), have been well known for centuries. François Villon (1431–c.1463) immortalized them in his 'Ballade des Femmes de Paris' in these lines:

> Prince, aux dames Parisiennes
> De beau parler donne le prix;
> Quoy qu'on die d'Italiennes,
> Il n'est bonbec que de Paris . . .'

## SOLE À LA BONNE FEMME (also for plaice, flounder, John Dory or any white fish)

8 large fish fillets (if possible keep the heads, skin etc. for stock)
2 heaped tablespoons butter
4 oz. (113 g.) mushrooms
½ tablespoon flour
¼ pint (½ cup) (0.142 l.) dry white wine

¼ pint (½ cup) (0.142 l.) fish stock or water
1 tablespoon lemon juice
1 tablespoon chopped parsley
a pinch of thyme
1 bayleaf
salt and freshly ground white pepper

If you have the heads, skin etc. of the fish then barely cover them with water, season to taste, add a bayleaf and a squeeze of lemon juice and simmer gently for about 40 minutes, then strain. Butter a large fireproof dish and well season the fish. Put a layer of chopped mushrooms mixed with parsley on the bottom then add the fillets. Pour over the wine and the stock or water, add the remainder of the herbs and half the lemon juice. Dot the top with a little butter cut in small pieces, then bring to boiling point, cover with foil or a lid and transfer to a moderate oven (350°F.) for about 10 minutes. Meanwhile sauté the remaining mushrooms very lightly in 1 tablespoon butter, adding seasoning and a dash of lemon juice. Work the flour into the remaining butter, take the fish from the oven and pour off the liquid into a small saucepan. Add the butter rolled in flour (*beurre manié*), heat and reduce until it has thickened slightly. Arrange the sautéed mushrooms on top of the fish, pour the reduced sauce over the top and glaze for a minute or two under a hot grill.

Serves 4.

SOLE VERONIQUE is made as above omitting the mushrooms, but 1 cup of seedless, peeled white grapes are added just before the fish is glazed.

*Fish stall at Les Halles market, rue Rambuteau, 1898.*

# GALETTES AU FROMAGE

On the left is 'Le Moulin Blute-Fin' and on the right 'Le Rader' mill, now both known by the one name 'Moulin de la Galette', and immortalized by Renoir in his painting 'Bal du Moulin de la Galette'. The Debray family were the millers of the 'Dames de L'Abbaye de Montmartre' since the sixteenth century. In 1814 after the capitulation of Paris (31st March), fighting continued in the heights of La Butte, and five men of the Debray family (four brothers and the only son of the eldest) fought the Russians. All perished in various inhuman ways except the son, who miraculously survived, although badly wounded. Some time later, unable to continue as a miller and being extremely fond of dancing, he transformed the mills into public dancing places, and for the rest of his life told the story of his survival. Alas, it no longer functions as such, although the Moulin Rader is now the little Théâtre du Tertre.

'We are in search of the Moulin de la Galette . . . and after many twistings and turnings . . . we see before us an old blackened windmill. It is the Moulin de la Galette. Beneath it there is a green wooden archway . . . through this we pass into a *salon* – with a polished floor, gaily decorated, and glistening with chandeliers; where all the lively scenes that one has read of in books on student life are to be expected.' Dorothy Menpes, *Paris,* 1909.

## GALETTES AU FROMAGE (Cheese wafers)

½ lb. (227 g.) Gruyère cheese
½ lb. (1 cup) (227 g.) soft
  butter
3 heaped tablespoons
  (approx.) sifted flour
pinch of cayenne pepper and
  black pepper
coffee-spoon dry mustard

TO GARNISH
1 egg
2 tablespoons grated
  Gruyère or Parmesan
  cheese

Combine all ingredients (except garnish) in a bowl and mix well, adding a little more flour if it is too sticky, but not more than a tablespoon. With floured hands break off about a tablespoon of the mixture and roll into a ball, then flatten slightly to about ¼ inch thick. Do this until all the mixture is used, putting them on to a greased and floured baking sheet, not too close together. Paint the tops with beaten egg and a sprinkle of cheese. Bake for 10–15 minutes in a hot oven (425°F.) until they have spread a little, puffed and are golden brown. Cool on a rack.
  Makes about 28.

*Moulin de la Galette, rue Lepic, Montmartre, c.1860.*

# POMMES DE TERRE À LA PARISIENNE

In 1826 the Scotsman Dr Robertson opened the pleasure gardens *(based on the English gardens such as Cremorne and Surrey) just off the boulevard de Clichy, called the New Tivoli. Apart from acrobats, jugglers and fireworks, many of Robertson's ingenious inventions such as the Phantascope, which he showed in his* Cabinet de Physique amusant *(chamber of amusing physics), and his hydraulic toys, fountains and water-works were on display and drew enormous crowds. He was the first person to light his gardens with gas. Together with his son Eugène he also organized and participated in several balloon ascents. In 1831 he installed a* Tir aux Pigeons *(see page 17). The gardens survived until 1841.*

*Utrillo painted many pictures of this quarter and in extreme poverty often slept on the benches. Picasso had his first* atelier *in the boulevard, and was a constant visitor to the cinema in the rue de Douai, where he enjoyed the films of George Méliès, as well as to the nearby Cirque Medrano, to which he went as often as three times a week during the period when he was painting his circus pictures. The Moulin Rouge (page 36) and the Cabaret de l'Enfer (page 82) as well as many other cafés frequented by writers, painters and* rapins *(young students apprenticed to a painter) are in the place Pigalle and the place Blanche just off the boulevard. Rissoles (known as* roinsolles *in the thirteenth century), which are chopped or minced meat enclosed in pastry and then deep fried, were popular with students and workmen. They were known as 'denrées aux dès' (dice food) as they were often used as stakes when playing dice in the cafés.*

## POMMES DE TERRE À LA PARISIENNE (Parisian potatoes)

Peel and wash 2 lb. (1 kg.) potatoes, then with a small potato scoop cut them into small balls the size of a small walnut. Soak for 1 hour, drain, then dry well. Sauté them in foaming, but not brown, butter until they are evenly golden, drain, and keep warm. Before serving put them in a pan with 1 cup meat jelly or consommé and toss them round well. Serve hot liberally sprinkled with chopped parsley.

Serves 6–8.

This is part of the garnish for dishes called *à la Parisienne*. When served simply sautéed they are called *Pommes de terre Noisette*.

*Flowerseller on boulevard de Clichy, Montmartre, c.1895. Photographer, Eugène Atget.*

# LE LOUP DE MER FLAMBÉ AU FENOUIL

The boulevard Montparnasse was well known in the eighteenth century for its guinguettes (see page 41), a popular one being La Grand-Chaumière, started in 1783 by an Englishman called Tickson who, with a French partner, laid out gardens, provided swings and switchbacks, built a two-storey house, and provided many fashionable amenities which attracted the painter Corot (who gave a banquet there) and many others. The Closerie des Lilas started as a guinguette in 1803 where students came to dance with grisettes, whose favourite things were 'switchbacks, lobster salad and the theatre'. In the late nineteenth century, when it was still surrounded by lilacs, it had become a café, the meeting place for Ingres, Châteaubriand, Verlaine, Henry James and the champions of Dreyfus. This tradition continued for almost a hundred years, but since the last war it is no longer a café: the open-air section has been enclosed to provide dining alcoves, and it is a first-class restaurant with a magnificent menu. One of the specialities is:

## LE LOUP DE MER FLAMBÉ AU FENOUIL

Recipe kindly given by Madame Milan, owner of La Closerie des Lilas. (Bass and sea bass, sometimes translated as sea-perch, with fennel, flambéed. Red mullet, sea bream, John Dory or snapper can also be used.)

| | |
|---|---|
| 1 large fish about 2½ lb. (1.135 kg.) | 6 dried fennel stalks |
| olive oil | 1 glass anise-based spirit such as Pernod; or brandy |
| salt and freshly ground pepper | |

Get the fishmonger to clean the fish, unless using red mullet, for the liver of this fish is considered a delicacy. For this reason red mullet (rouget in French) is known as the 'woodcock of the sea'. Scrape the larger scales from the skin then paint the fish all over with olive oil, rubbing in coarse salt and freshly ground pepper to taste. Put on to a grilling pan and grill on each side for about 7 minutes: do not have the grill too hot for this will burn the skin and leave the fish undercooked inside if it is a thick one. Warm a large fireproof serving dish and arrange the fennel twigs on it, then put the cooked fish on top. Warm the spirit in a small ladle, pour over and set light to it. When the flames have died down the fish is ready and will have a delectable smell and flavour of fennel. The flaming can be done in the kitchen or at table, whichever is more convenient. Madame Milan serves a Pernod-flavoured béarnaise sauce with this dish, but personally I prefer a thick wedge of lemon.

Serves 4.

La Closerie des Lilas, boulevard Montparnasse, c.1922.

59

# POTAGE LONGCHAMPS

*The farm of Longchamps was pulled down in the 1850s to make a review ground and later racecourse (see page 22). The inauguration of the racecourse was on Sunday 26th April 1857 in the presence of the Emperor, the Empress and the Grand Duke Constantine.*

'At a French race, nine-tenths of the men go there merely because it is fashionable and because it is a more exciting way of killing time than sitting in a club reading newspapers. And as for the women, it is an opportunity for showing off a "fast", but be it confessed, a becoming toilet . . . of the true spirit of the affair the French comprehend not one iota.' *Reminiscences and Recollections of Captain Gronow*, vol. 2, 1860s. '. . . the breeding of bloodstock has occupied the attention of many Frenchmen, and has been attended with no small success . . .' ibid.

In 1865 Gladiateur owned by the Comte de Lagrange was the first French horse to win the Epsom Derby; also the Grand Prix de Paris at Longchamps; the 'Triple Crown'; le Prix Nobel; the 2,000 Guineas, and the St Leger all in the same year. The first Grand Prix was run in 1863 and won by an English horse, The Ranger. M. William, a colourful racecourse celebrity of the period, when asked how he obtained the magnificent shine on his *haut-de-forme*, maintained that he made his valet run for half-an-hour, then wiped off the sweat with a foulard handkerchief and polished his hat with it . . .

'one must have clean healthy fellow . . . as blond as possible, as all sweats won't do. I gave the recipe to the Prince of Wales.'

## POTAGE LONGCHAMPS

A classical French soup can be simply made by combining 1 quart (1.142 l.) fresh (or 2 cans) green pea soup with $1\frac{1}{4}$ pints ($2\frac{1}{2}$ cups) (0.71 l.) consommé. It is garnished with a *chiffonade* of sorrel leaves (sorrel lightly softened in butter), a little vermicelli and fresh, chopped chervil.

Serves 8–10.

## ŒUFS JOCKEY-CLUB (Jockey Club Eggs)

Consist of fried eggs, trimmed with a cutter so that only a small band of white remains, set on toast spread with *foie gras* (liver pâté) around a large serving plate. The middle is filled with finely sliced veal kidney cooked in butter and moistened with Madeira. A small sliver of truffle is placed on each egg.

*Watching a military review, Longchamps racecourse, c.1892.*

# CÔTES DE VEAUX AUX FINES HERBES

The old nobility of France used to be known in French slang as 'Le Gratin', *from which no doubt, comes the English expression* 'the upper crust', *and the American one* 'the big cheese', *a* gratin *being the thin glazed crust, with or without cheese, obtained by putting certain dishes under a hot grill. The* 'Gratin' *lived in the Faubourg Saint-Germain quarter, bordered on the north by the Seine, the south by the* quartier Saint François Xavier, *the east by the* rue des Saint-Pères *and on the west by the Avenue de la Bourdonnais. Sainte-Clothilde was the church at which they worshipped. Madame de Gramont called the quarter* 'a fortified region to which few have access . . .' *and continued :* 'The frivolity of the woman of the 18th century was ransomed by the austerity of their 19th century descendants,' *for although they lived in grand style,* '. . . they were anything but hospitable'.

## CÔTES DE VEAUX AUX FINES HERBES  (veal chops with herbs)

| | |
|---|---|
| 4 trimmed veal chops | 1 tablespoon of mixed |
| 2 tablespoons butter | chopped tarragon and |
| 1 tablespoon olive oil | chervil |
| 1 small chopped shallot | 1 tablespoon chopped parsley |
| $\frac{1}{8}$ pint ($\frac{1}{4}$ cup) (71 ml.) | 6 tablespoons meat jelly or |
| white wine | consommé |
| | salt and freshly ground pepper |

Heat the butter and oil until foaming but not coloured then sauté the chops on both sides in it, until golden brown and well cooked. Transfer to a warmed serving dish and keep hot. Add the finely chopped shallot to the pan together with the white wine, scraping down the sides of the pan and mixing well. Then add the jelly or consommé, salt and pepper, and bring to the boil. Simmer for 2 minutes, then add the herbs, stir well and pour over the chops.

Serves 4.

*Dining-room of the Duc de La Rochefoucauld-Doudeauville, rue de Varenne, c.1890s.*

# Œ UFS BONNE FEMME

The heights of Belleville were known as the Haute-Courtille, courtille *meaning a house with a garden in old French. The rue de Belleville was famous for its* guinguettes *(page 41) and a remarkable carnival which took place for three days, ending on Ash Wednesday. All classes of people from duchesses to provincials rented seats, as early as a month ahead, and every available carriage, fiacre and barouche was hired to bring them there. The workers economized all the year round to enjoy this three day carnival. Everywhere was bursting with people, the* guingettes *and cabarets (page 82) filled up the night before. In the streets bonbons were thrown and when they finished, eggs full of flour (a joke invented by* mitrons, *young baker's apprentices, and the forerunner no doubt of the custard-pie comedy) were thrown, fruit, vegetables, anything to hand. Extempore performances were given, and fishwives had broadsheets of risqué retorts printed. The rich who had not abandoned their carriages finished at the 'Vendanges de Bourgogne' tavern. Custom decreed that all vessels were broken after each meal, for which the company paid, therefore only cracked china was used, thus giving a bigger margin of profit for the tavern-keeper. During the course of the meal the ladies were pelted with sugared almonds and they retaliated by drenching the men in champagne and throwing oyster shells.*

*It is somehow difficult to reconcile this three-day rout with the neat, clean little room of the photograph, although there are several carnival favours decorating the walls. The large* marmite

*on the stove undoubtedly contained* Pot-au-feu *(page 13) which, alternating with eggs, cheese and bread, was no doubt her everyday menu.*

## ŒUFS BONNE FEMME (Baked eggs with mushrooms)

| | |
|---|---|
| 8 eggs | ½ lb. (227 g.) mushrooms |
| 8 circles approx. 4 inches across of thick white bread | 3 tablespoons grated cheese chopped parsley for garnish |
| 6 tablespoons butter | |
| salt and freshly ground pepper | |

Heat up half the butter and fry the bread on both sides in it until a pale gold, then arrange closely in an ovenproof dish. Heat the remaining butter and very lightly soften the chopped mushrooms, but do not let them get crisp. Season to taste, then put them on top of the croûtons. Carefully break an egg over each croûton, sprinkle with salt and pepper and a little grated cheese. Put into a moderate oven (350°F.) for about 10 minutes until the whites are set and the yolks soft. Garnish with a little chopped parsley.

Serves 4.

*A working girl's bed-sitting room, rue de Belleville, c.1882.*

# STEAK AU POIVRE

*Sasha was the actor son of Lucien Guitry, one of France's most famous and well-loved actors who was also an actor-manager, for after leaving the Comédie Française he took over the management of the Théâtre de la Renaissance. Amongst many other parts, he played Sergeant Flambeau to Sarah Bernhardt's l'Aiglon and was her ardent admirer. Tristan Bernard was a successful dramatist known for his gentleness and bon mots. 'Love affairs are like mushrooms. One doesn't know if they're the safe or poisonous variety until it's too late.' Sasha Guitry called him 'Paris's best-loved and fullest-bearded wit.'*

## STEAK AU POIVRE (Pepper steak)

| | |
|---|---|
| 4 trimmed sirloin or fillet (tenderloin) steaks | 8 tablespoons bouillon or red wine |
| 3 tablespoons crushed peppercorns | 3 tablespoons brandy |
| 3 tablespoons butter | fresh watercress for garnish, optional |
| 1 tablespoon olive oil | |

Crush the peppercorns in a mortar, or put into waxed paper and roll until powdered. Divide among the steaks and press over both sides of the meat and leave to stand, if possible, for at least ½ hour. Heat up 2 tablespoons butter and the oil then sauté the steaks on each side, for several minutes according to taste. Remove steaks and keep warm. Pour the bouillon in to the pan, bring to boiling point and reduce to half the quantity. Put the steaks back in pan, add the warmed brandy and set it alight. Add remaining butter in small pieces until it is well amalgamated with the pan juices. Serve at once with garnish.

Enough for 4.

BŒUF À LA FICELLE is the speciality of two Paris restaurants (Marie-Louise, rue Championnet, 18e, and Cartet, 62, rue de Malte, 11e). A beef fillet or *faux-filet* (sirloin) is tightly secured with string and roasted in a hot oven (425°F.) for 7–10 minutes to the pound or browned in a pan. It is then dropped by the string into boiling consommé or bouillon to cover it well, for 12 to 15 minutes. This makes for very tender and succulent beef, but the meat must be in a joint, not individual steaks, and rolled tightly into a sausage shape about 3 inches in diameter.

*Actor Sasha Guitry (in stripes) with Tristan Bernard and other friends, 1913.*

# COQUILLES AUX ASPERGES

*Claude Monet was born in Paris and after a short spell spent in the army in Africa, where he contracted fever, he entered the atelier of the classical painter Gleyre, from whom he broke away after meeting Sisley and Renoir. In 1869 he joined a group which included Cézanne and Degas. During the war of 1870 he went to England, where he painted many beautiful river scenes of London. On his return he went to live at Argenteuil, near Paris. One of his most famous paintings is 'Le Dejeuner sur l'herbe'.*

*Argenteuil is noted for growing the finest asparagus in France, fat and white almost to the tips; when a dish is called Argenteuil it always contains asparagus.*

'One fine day in the month of February, walking through the Palais-Royal, I stopped before the shop of Madame Chevet . . . who has always been extremely kind to me; noticing a bundle of asparagus, the thinnest of which was fatter than my index finger, I asked her the price of it. "Forty francs, Monsieur" ". . . at such a price no-one but the King or some prince will be able to eat them." "You are mistaken; such luxuries never find their way into palaces; . . . kings want goodness, not magnificence . . ." As she was talking, two fat Englishmen stopped in front of us . . . one of them had the miraculous bundle wrapped up without so much as asking the price . . . and carried it off, whistling "God Save the King".' Brillat-Savarin, *La Physiologie du Goût*, 1825.

## COQUILLES AUX ASPERGES
### (Scalloped Asparagus)

16 thick asparagus heads
2 tablespoons butter
2 tablespoons flour
½ pint (1 cup) (0.285 l.) warm milk
4 oz. (113 g.) tongue or ham, chopped

12 button mushrooms, chopped
4 heaped tablespoons grated Gruyère cheese
pinch nutmeg
4 tablespoons breadcrumbs
salt and pepper

Scrape and trim the asparagus if fresh and cook in boiling salted water for 20 minutes, then drain carefully and remove any hard stalk when cooled. Just soften the mushrooms in half the butter and remove, then heat the remaining butter, stir in the flour, cook for 1 minute then add the milk, stirring all the time, until thick. Off the heat add all other ingredients except the breadcrumbs, and season to taste. Divide into 4 or 6 scallop shells, or small dishes, sprinkle the crumbs over and brown in a hot oven (400°F.) for about 20 minutes.

Serves 4–6.

*Claude Monet (1840–1926), the Impressionist painter, in his atelier, 1924.*

# DARNES DE SAUMON GLACÉES PARISIENNE

*Only the French could think of giving a banquet for 23,000 people. Practically the whole of the rue de Rivoli and the Place du Carousel were tented over for it. The catering was done by Potel & Chabot, still France's leading catering firm.*

## DARNES DE SAUMON GLACÉES PARISIENNE (Cold salmon steaks Parisian style)

6 salmon steaks about
  2 inches thick, or in one
  piece, approx. 3 lb.
  (1.36 kg.)
fish trimmings if possible
½ pint (1 cup) (0.285 l.) white
  wine and the same of water
2 chopped shallots or 1 small
  onion

1 tablespoon butter
2 sprigs parsley
1 tablespoon lemon juice
salt and pepper
2 cups fresh mayonnaise
  beaten with ½ cup cooled
  aspic or fish jelly

Put the fish trimmings, bones etc. if any, shallots, lemon juice, herbs, salt and pepper into a saucepan, add the white wine and water, bring to the boil and simmer for about 1 hour. Cool slightly and strain. Heat the butter and lightly turn the salmon steaks in it, not letting them colour. Put them into the boiling *court bouillon*, cover with buttered paper or foil and poach very gently, hardly letting the water tremble, for about ½ hour. Cool in the water. When cool, take out, remove the skin, and if serving masked with the sauce, take each side fillet from the bones, seeing that no small ones are left. Arrange on the serving dish. When chilled the fish liquor should be jellied; if not, use 1 level tablespoon of aspic to ½ pint (1 cup) (0.285 l.) stock. Make the mayonnaise and when the aspic stock is cool, but still liquid, beat this quickly into the mayonnaise. Pour over the steaks straight away as it will set very quickly. Serve cold, garnished with asparagus tips, cooked French beans, and tiny green peas arranged in small heaps around the fish.

Serves 6.

*Section of tent for banquet of 23,000 mayors given by the President of the French Republic, rue de Rivoli, 22nd September 1900.* 71

# JAMBON BRAISÉ AU MADÈRE

*Sardou was a highly successful playwright and intimate friend of Sarah Bernhardt (page 74) for whom he wrote many plays which they produced jointly. George Bernard Shaw referred to these slick, contrived plays as 'sheer Sardoudledum'. Théodora, with music by Massenet, netted over two and a half million francs on its first run at the Odéon theatre. He had a phobia about draughts, winter and summer, and always wore a hat, even in the house.*

## JAMBON BRAISÉ AU MADÈRE (Ham braised with Madeira)

*Jambon de Paris* or *Jambon glacé* is used in France.

| | |
|---|---|
| 1 raw ham 8–10 lb. (4–5 kg.) | ½ pint (1 cup) (0.285 l.) Madeira wine |
| 1½ bottles dry white wine | |
| 2½ pints (5 cups) (1½ l.) water or stock | 2 cups ham stock |
| 4 large sliced carrots | 1 pint (2 cups) (0.57 l.) |
| 2 large sliced onions | Sauce Brune (see page 95) |
| 1 bayleaf | 6 tablespoons Madeira |
| bouquet garni of herbs | |
| 2 sprigs parsley | |
| 6 peppercorns and 3 cloves | |

Soak the ham overnight in cold water, take out and scrape the skin with a knife. Put the wine, water, carrots, onions, herbs and seasoning into a large saucepan, bring to the boil and simmer for about 30 minutes. Put the ham in skin side up, bring to the boil, then lower the heat until the water is just shuddering slightly. Cook for 3–3½ hours, let it cool, then take out and remove the skin, and a certain amount of the fat if it is very fatty. Let the stock get cold and remove fat from the top. Put the ham into a large ovenproof dish, add the cup of Madeira wine and 2 cups of ham stock (taste first to ensure it is not too salty; if it is, dissolve a stock cube instead) and bake in a moderate oven (375°F.) for about 45 minutes basting frequently with the liquid. Turn out the oven and leave for at least 15 minutes before putting on to a warmed serving dish with some of the braising liquid, and keep warm. This makes carving much easier.

While the ham is in the oven, reduce the Sauce Brune to almost half, then add the 6 tablespoons Madeira, heat but do not re-boil. Put into a sauceboat and serve separately. Chambertin or a similar wine can be used instead of Madeira if liked.

Serves about 16–20.

PETITS POIS À LA FRANÇAISE (peas cooked in the French style) make a good accompaniment to the ham, and are prepared as follows. Put 6 cups shelled small green peas into a saucepan with a shredded lettuce heart, 12 small chopped onions, a *bouquet garni*, ½ cup butter, 3 teaspoons sugar, seasonings and 4 tablespoons water. Cover and simmer for about ½ hour, when the liquid will be almost absorbed.

*Playwright Victorien Sardou (1831–1908) dining at home with his wife, mother, daughters and son, c.1890.*

# FRAISES À LA SARAH BERNHARDT

Sarah Bernhardt (born Rosine Bernard in Paris), France's and *possibly the world's greatest tragic actress, was also a dynamic and remarkable character. Sardou said of her: 'If there's anything more astonishing than to watch Sarah Bernhardt act, it's to watch her live.' She possessed untiring energy even in old age, and when her friends commented on it she replied: 'Rest? With all eternity before me?' She attributed her energy to being able to sleep for very short periods and awaken refreshed. Many of these 'cat-naps' were taken in her rosewood, satin-lined flower-strewn coffin, which was kept in her boudoir, and much publicized, with the lighted candle and grinning skull on the floor adding to the dramatic effect. As well as being a great actress she also sculpted and painted in no mean fashion, kept a menagerie of wild and domestic animals in her apartment on the boulevard Péreire as well as in her summer house at Belle-Isle-en-Mer. Unpredictable in everything, especially food, she nevertheless had many dishes named after her: one of her favourite restaurants was L'Escargot – Montorgueil (page 19), where the ceiling fresco from her summer house is installed in her memory.*

## FRAISES À LA SARAH BERNHARDT
(Strawberries à la Sarah Bernhardt)

| | |
|---|---|
| 2 lb. (1 kg.) strawberries | ½ lb. (227 g.) puréed strawberries |
| 6 tablespoons each brandy and Curaçao | ½ pint (1 cup) (0.285 l.) cream, whipped |
| 2 cups pineapple water-ice | 1 tablespoon Curaçao |

Wash and hull the strawberries, then put the 2 lb. into the serving dish and cover with the 6 tablespoons brandy and Curaçao. Leave to macerate for several hours, turning over so that all are soaked in the spirits. Purée the remaining strawberries and shortly before it is needed whip the cream, add the tablespoon of Curaçao to the purée and mix well. Just before serving, put the pineapple ice on top of the strawberries, mix the purée with the whipped cream and put on top in small peaks.

Serves 4–6.

'It was Monsieur le Comte de la Place who discovered a very special way of treating strawberries, by sprinkling them with the juice of a sweet orange (the apple of Hesperides). Another savant has further improved on this recipe by adding the outer rind of the orange, which he rubs off with a lump of sugar; he claims to have proved, through a fragment of manuscript saved from the torches which destroyed the library of Alexandria, that this was the way strawberries were seasoned at the banquets on Mount Ida.' Brillat-Savarin, *La Physiologie du Goût,* 1825.

*Sarah Bernhardt – 'The Divine Sarah' – (1844–1923), in her coffin-bed, c.1860s.*

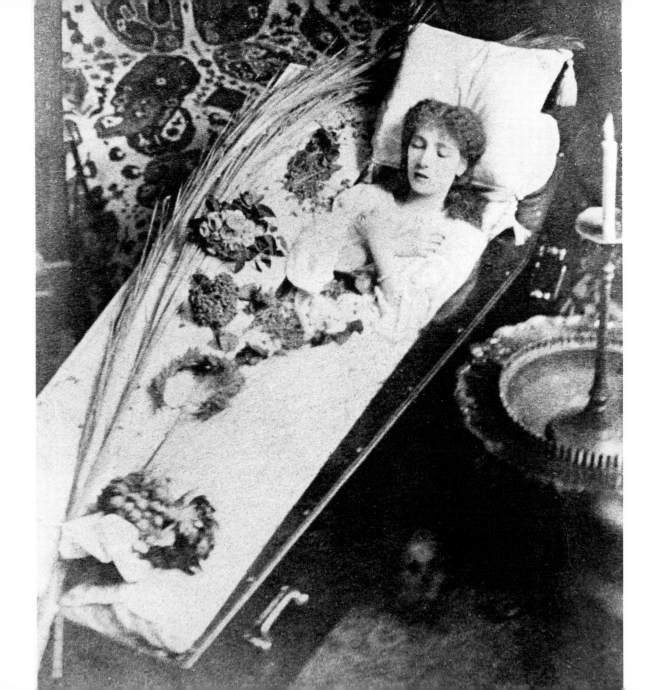

# OMELETTE À LA PARISIENNE

The Lapin Agile was a famous café frequented by Picasso, Max Jacob, Apollinaire, Modigliani, Severini, Poulbot, Utrillo and many other artists of the period. It was previously a traiteur (page 1) called the 'Cabaret des Assassins', a name given from the many bloody fights which took place when it was an inn for horse-lorry drivers. When Frédéric (Frédé) Gérard (who had been a street fish-seller before he became patron) took over with his pet donkey, Lolo, the entire atmosphere changed. He was a large, jovial man, a born entertainer who amused his clients with extempore poems and songs accompanied by his guitar. It was situated at the cross of the rue des Saules and the rue St Vincent, which at that time was a country district. Ironically, the ex-Cabaret des Assassins lived up to its name when Frédé's son was murdered there by an unknown person, and legend has it that, with tears streaming down his face, Frédé played his guitar.

GROG is a popular drink in Paris on a cold day.

Put a good measure of pale rum in a tumbler, add 1 teaspoon of sugar, 3 cloves and a wedge of lemon. Top up with boiling water and stir well.

## OMELETTE À LA PARISIENNE WITH SAUCE BERCY

8 eggs
3 tablespoons butter
1 medium chopped onion
6 medium mushrooms
½ lb. (227 g.) chipolata
  sausages
salt and pepper

SAUCE BERCY*
3 finely chopped shallots
½ pint (1 cup) (0.285 l.) dry
  white wine
3 tablespoons butter
squeeze of lemon juice
1 teaspoon chopped parsley
salt and pepper

First make the sauce by simmering the shallots in the wine until it is reduced by half, stir in the good squeeze of lemon juice, season and add the butter in small pieces. Do not reboil, but reheat and garnish with parsley. Grill the sausages and meanwhile make the omelette. Sauté the onion in 1 tablespoon of butter until soft and golden, then drain. Using another tablespoon of butter sauté the mushrooms very lightly and drain. Add onions and mushrooms to the lightly beaten eggs, heat the remaining butter and cook the omelette in the usual way. Serve hot from the pan with the sausages on top and the sauce poured around like a ring. Eat with hot, crusty bread.

Serves 2.

*Sauce Bercy can be served with eggs, fish, liver and steak.

Frédé entertains Francique Poulbot the painter and his friends at the Lapin Agile, Montmartre, 1905.

# POMMES DE TERRE ANNA

*One of the most famous Paris restaurants, which opened in 1802, was renowned for its private dining-room on the second floor, called 'le Salon de Grand Seize', reserved exclusively for royalty to entertain their friends of the demi-monde. Courtesans such as La Belle Otero, Liane de Pougy, Emilienne d'Alençon (they were known as Les Grandes Trois) were all constant visitors, as was Cora Pearl (see page 81). It is said that at the end of one of the dinners in Le Grand Seize, four waiters entered to a fanfare of music and carrying an enormous covered serving dish which was put in the centre of the table. When the lid was taken off Cora Pearl was lying naked in the middle, some say covered with a pink sauce, others, nature. True or not it gives an indication of the usual festivities. Nevertheless the Café Anglais did not rely entirely on spectacle, for it employed excellent chefs such as Dugléré, who created Sole Dugléré; also other dishes such as Potage Germiny (made from beef consommé, sorrel, chervil, butter and cream all thickened with egg-yolks) and Pommes de Terre Anna. M. Claude Terrail who owns La Tour d'Argent (page 9) is the grandson of the last owner of the Café Anglais.*

'To the Café Anglais did they accordingly repair; and in a few minutes a dish of oysters – a lobster – a broiled fowl – and an omelette aux fines herbes were ready for their discussion in a *cabinet particulier* . . .' G. W. M. Reynolds, *Pickwick Abroad or the Tour in France*, 1839.

*Café Anglais, c.1912 : the café closed in 1913.*

## POMMES DE TERRE ANNA (Potatoes Anna)

| | |
|---|---|
| 2 lb. (1 kg.) potatoes, peeled and sliced | 6 oz. ($\frac{3}{4}$ cup) (170 g.) butter salt and freshly ground pepper |

Put the peeled and thinly sliced potatoes to stand in cold water for at least half an hour. Drain and dry well in a cloth. Butter a fairly deep ovenproof dish all over, then put a layer of potatoes on the bottom, season to taste, and cover with a layer of softened butter. Repeat until the dish is full, ending with a layer of butter. Cover and bake in a moderate oven (375°F.) for about 40 minutes. At the end of that time, take out of the oven, remove the lid, turn the 'cake'. Return, uncovered, to the oven for a further 15 minutes or until the potatoes are cooked through. Invert on to a heated serving dish and serve hot.

Serves 4–6.

# HOMARDS À LA NAGE

*Cora Pearl, one of the most famous courtesans of 'La Belle Epoque', was an Irish girl, born Emma Crouch, daughter of the song-writer who gave us 'Kathleen Mavourneen'. One of her many 'protectors' was Prince Napoleon, son of King Jérôme. See also page 79. She is seen here wearing a crinoline, the innovation of the Englishman Charles Worth (1825–95) who became one of the finest dress designers in the world. Edmond de Goncourt wrote in his Journal, 11th January 1872: '. . . noticed a throng of private carriages quite as great as one would see outside the Théâtre Français on a first night. . . . was wondering who the great personage could be . . . when, raising my eyes above the entrance, I read WORTH.' Worth dressed the Empress Eugénie, Queen Victoria, French and Russian nobility, but his favourite clients were Americans because, he said, 'they loved all clothes and had faith, figures and francs'.*

The famous restaurant Maxim's, still in the grand tradition in the Rue Royale, was a showcase for many of the spectacular courtesans of the time.

## HOMARDS À LA NAGE (Lobsters in the swim)
Recipe kindly given by Madame L. Vaudable of Maxim's Restaurant

6 live lobsters (about 1¼ lb. (½ kg.) each)

3 coffee-spoons rock salt
½ lb. (1 cup) (227 g.) butter

2 finely chopped carrots
1 finely chopped medium onion
6 cloves garlic
1 bottle dry white wine

½ lemon
1 chopped celery stalk
bouquet garni of herbs
2 teaspoons coarsely ground black pepper

Put the peeled and chopped carrots, onions, celery, garlic (unpeeled and whole), bouquet garni, salt, pepper and white wine into a pot (large enough to hold the lobsters) three-quarters full of water. Wash and rinse the lobsters, and put into the pot, cover, and bring slowly to the boil and simmer for 15 minutes. Meanwhile mix the softened butter with the juice of the lemon and season it with salt and pepper, beat it vigorously and set aside. Remove the lobsters and take about a quarter of the stock, including the carrots, onions and 2 or 3 of the garlic cloves and keep hot. Split the lobsters in half longways, extract the meat, discarding the intestines and crop. Place the meat from body and the claws either in a hot serving dish or 6 soup bowls. Cover the meat with some of the cooked vegetables. Pour into a sauceboat a little of the stock and mix with the prepared butter to make the sauce, which should be served separately.

Serves 6.

*Cora Pearl, c.1860. Photographer, A. Disdéri.*

# PÊCHES À LA DIABLE

*The meaning of the word* cabaret *has changed considerably, for originally it was simply a place at which to eat and drink, the oldest known* cabaret *being* La Pomme de Pin *opened in 1400, where 'today one of the pavilions of the* Hôtel-Dieu *stands. It was frequented by Rabelais, Villon, Molière, Racine and many others. The proprietor needed a certificate from his guild, the municipality, and the King's Attorney. He was allowed only five days holiday a year, and those who sold drink could remain open. Rather like early London coffee-houses, people of one trade or profession congregated in their own* cabaret *and would not frequent another.*

'The cafés and *cabarets* of Montmartre are different . . . there are cabarets of Heaven, Hell and Death, where the waiters are dressed respectively as angels, devils, undertakers. The Montmartrois find pleasure in combining merriment with death; they like to chuck the devil under the chin. You enter the cabaret of Heaven through Golden Gates . . . the angel Gabriel guards the entrance, an angel with an ill-shaven face . . . You dine . . . accompanied by solemn church music; garçons dressed as seraphs, the proprietor, clothed as a priest, addresses you from the pulpit . . . when you call for a drink, the ferocious angel at your elbow growls, "Thy will be done". For quite a small sum, anyone can float up and down through ethereal space along with a bevy of angels.'

Dorothy Menpes, *Paris*, 1909.

## PÊCHES À LA DIABLE (Devilled peaches)

| | |
|---|---|
| 2 sponge cakes 8 inches in diameter | 4 stiffly beaten egg-whites |
| 10 medium peaches, peeled and pitted | 4 tablespoons fine sugar |
| 8 tablespoons Kirsch | 2 tablespoons chopped or ground almonds |

Cut the peeled peaches in half and soak in 6 tablespoons of Kirsch. Beat the egg-whites with the sugar until stiff, finally adding the ground almonds. Arrange the peach halves with their juice on top of the 2 sponge cakes and cover both with the beaten egg-white. Put into a moderate oven (375°F.) for about 15–20 minutes until the meringue is golden brown. Just before serving, warm the remaining Kirsch, pour over and ignite.

Serves 6–8.

*Cabaret de l'Enfer (Hell), boulevard de Clichy, Montmartre, 1900. Nearby was the Cabaret du Ciel (Heaven).*

# MADELEINES

*The Château de Bagatelle was built for Jean d'Estrées, Marshal and Vice-Admiral of France, nephew of Gabrielle d'Estrées, a mistress of Henry IV. In 1835 Lord Yarmouth (later Marquis of Hertford) bought it and it passed to Sir Richard Wallace, the Marquis's illegitimate son by the Scottish girl Agnes Wallace. Wallace was created a baronet in 1871 in recognition of the help he had given to the English colony in Paris during the Siege of 1871. He inherited Lord Hertford's fine collection of paintings and his large estate in recognition of his kindness to Lord Hertford and his mother. In 1871 Sir Richard gave eighty fountains, sculptured by Lebourg, to the Town of Paris, many of which are in the Luxembourg Gardens. He married a French girl and predeceased her by seven years. On her death she left all the paintings and contents of Hertford House to the English nation; this gift is now known as the Wallace Collection.*

MADELEINES (small, light shell-shaped cakes originally from Commercy, the taste of which, dipped in tea, begins the long journey into the past made by the French writer, Marcel Proust).

Madeleine moulds are oval in shape and ridged on the bottom: however, any fluted tartlet mould can be used.

| | |
|---|---|
| ½ lb. (1 cup) (227 g.) fine sugar | ½ lb. (1 cup) (227 g.) melted butter |
| ½ lb. (2 cups) (227 g.) sifted cake flour | pinch of salt |
| finely grated rind 1 lemon | 1 beaten egg-white |
| 4 eggs | icing (confectioners') sugar |

First lightly butter and flour about 20 moulds. Then mix together the flour, sugar and salt in a bowl, adding the eggs one by one and beating very thoroughly. (Use an electric mixer if possible as this makes them very light.) Then stir in lightly, the lemon rind grated very finely, and finally add the lukewarm melted butter, seeing that it is very well-mixed. Fill the prepared moulds two-thirds full, and bake in a moderate oven (375°F.) for about 25 minutes, or until risen and well-browned. Brush with beaten egg-white and dust with icing sugar and put back in a very low oven for 5 minutes to dry out.
    Makes about 20.

*Sir Richard Wallace, the Marquis of Hertford and Lady Hertford, Château de Bagatelle, Bois de Boulogne, c.1860s.*

# TARTE TATIN

*In 1612 the Luxembourg Palace and gardens were bought from the Duc de Luxembourg by Marie de Medici for her private use. The park was enormous, covering the present boulevard St Michel and the rue Notre Dames-des-Champs.*

'I loitered in the Luxembourg Gardens to watch the birds and the sunlight . . . and began to wonder if there was anything better in the world worth doing than to sit in an alley of limes smoking, thinking of Paris and myself.' George Moore, *Memoirs of My Dead Life,* 1906.

## TARTE TATIN (French apple tart)

2½ lb. (1.135 kg.) eating apples
3½ oz. (½ cup) (100 g.) caster (extra-fine) sugar
3½ oz. (½ cup) (100 g.) butter

½ lb. (227 g.) puff pastry (use half quantities of recipe on page 49)

First make the pastry according to instructions on page 49, and roll out to fit an 8-inch shallow glass baking dish. Peel and core the apples and cut them into thickish slices. Put the butter and sugar in a flat, heavy (copper if possible) *sauteuse* or saucepan, arrange the apples on top and cook on a quick heat until the sugar has caramelized. Put them into the buttered baking dish, dampen the edges slightly with cold water and lay the pastry round over the top, pressing very gently around the edges. Make a small slit on top then put into a hot oven (450°F.) for 7 minutes, reducing the heat after that to 375°F. for 25–30 minutes longer, or until the top is golden. Remove from the oven, and straight away loosen the crust all round, put the plate it will be served from on top and turn the whole tart over so that the caramelized apple is on top. This tart is served warm with chilled whipped cream or Chantilly.
Serves 4–6.

## CRÈME CHANTILLY

Leave ½ pint (1 cup) (0.285 l.) cream overnight in the refrigerator. When needed, put into a very cold basin and beat until it has doubled in volume. Gradually add 2 tablespoons caster (extra-fine) sugar and beat again.

*Children playing in the Luxembourg Gardens, c.1890s.*

# BLANQUETTE DE VEAU

*The* Plat du Jour *in a café such as the one in the photograph can always be consumed on the premises or taken out to be eaten at home, so it is usually a dish which will not spoil in reheating.*

## BLANQUETTE DE VEAU (Creamy veal stew)

| | |
|---|---|
| 4 lb. (approx. 2 kg.) breast or shoulder of veal | 3 sprigs parsley |
| 2½ pints (1½ l.) veal stock or stock and water | 1 sprig thyme |
| 1 large onion | 18 button onions |
| 4 medium carrots | 18 button mushrooms simmered in 2 tablespoons butter and a squeeze of lemon |
| 2 leeks | |
| 1 bayleaf | salt and freshly ground pepper |
| 1 stalk celery | |

FOR THE ROUX*

| | |
|---|---|
| 2 tablespoons each of butter and flour | a pinch of nutmeg or mace |
| 2 egg-yolks | juice of ½ lemon |
| 4 tablespoons cream | 1 pint (2 cups) (0.57 l.) veal stock |

Trim the meat of skin, fat or gristle (the skin, gristle, bone, etc. can be simmered in water for 1 hour to make the veal stock) and cut it into 1-inch cubes, then soak it for 1 hour in cold water. Drain and pat it dry. Put the meat into a large heatproof casserole, cover with the stock, or stock and water, salt and pepper, then bring to the boil. Take off any scum which forms with a slotted spoon: when the top has a creamy texture, stop skimming. Add the large onion, chopped carrots, leeks, celery and herbs, cover and either simmer very gently on top of the stove, or put into a moderate to low oven (225°F.) for about 1½ hours or until the meat is tender. Check that the liquid is not running too low; if necessary add a little more water or stock.

Meanwhile, simmer the button onions in very little stock or water with seasonings until they are cooked, but firm: also heat the butter and simmer the mushrooms with the squeeze of lemon, for no longer than 5 minutes.

Take out the meat and ladle out 1 pint (2 cups) (0.57 l.) strained stock. Drain the veal, clean the casserole, put the meat back, and keep warm with the drained onions and mushrooms. Heat the butter for the *roux*, stir in the flour and cook for 1 minute, then add the warm veal stock and stir until it is smooth and creamy. Simmer slowly for 15 minutes. Take from the heat, and stir in the beaten egg-yolks, cream, nutmeg or mace, and lemon juice, heating to just under boiling point and stirring all the time. Pour this over the veal, onions and mushrooms, mixing well, and keep covered in a low oven until ready to serve. *Blanquette de veau* is usually served with boiled rice.

Enough for 6–8.

*It is sometimes made without the egg-yolks, in which case increase the butter and flour for the roux, by 1 tablespoon each.

88

*Workmen outside a café, boulevard Ménilmontant, c.1890.*

# ESCALOPES DE DINDE À LA CRÈME

*Among the many houses in this street several are worthy of note: number 4, l'Hôtel des Mousquetaires, is where d'Artagnan of* The Three Musketeers *lived; next door to the Hôtel de France is number 52, Hôtel de Trudon, the former home of M. Trudon the* sommelier *of Louis XV; and facing the fountain is l'Hôtel de François Barnom, who was Louis XIV's barber. The Hôtel de France was at one time a well known* maison d'assignation. *The name 'arbre-sec' possibly comes from the fact that a gibbet once stood in the street.*

## ESCALOPES DE DINDE À LA CRÈME (Turkey breasts with cream)

This recipe can also be used for escalope of veal, sliced pork fillet or boned chicken breasts. Turkey breast escalopes are very popular in Paris today. They are cooked excellently at Chez Raymonde, 3 rue Thérèse, 1er, at a most modest price.

8 thick slices raw turkey
  breast
3 tablespoons butter or oil
1 glass dry white wine
2 egg-yolks
juice of ½ lemon
1 heaped teaspoon tarragon
  mustard

4 oz. (113 g.) button
  mushrooms
¼ pint (½ cup) (0.142 l.)
  cream
salt and freshly ground
  white pepper

Heat the butter or oil and lightly fry the turkey escalopes on both sides, but do not colour, remove and keep them warm. Mix the mustard with the wine. Then lightly sauté the mushrooms in the butter, put back the turkey breasts, add seasonings, lemon juice, wine and the cream. Simmer very gently for 10–15 minutes and let it cool. Just before serving beat the egg-yolks with 1 tablespoon of the cooled sauce, heat up the turkey escalopes and sauce, and immediately before serving add the egg-yolk mixture, stir, reheat, but do not reboil.

Serves 4.

Braised endive (chicory in Britain) is an excellent accompaniment.

## ENDIVES À LA PARISIENNE

Trim 12 heads endive (chicory), removing the inner core of the bottom to avoid bitterness. Put side by side in a well-buttered casserole and pour around 1 cup consommé. Season to taste, dot with butter and add a good squeeze of lemon juice. Bake in a moderate oven (350°F.) for about 1 hour, turning once, or simmer slowly on top of the stove for ½ hour.

*Hôtel de France, rue de l'Arbre Sec, 1916. Photographer, Eugène Atget.*

# PÂTÉ CHAUD DE VEAU À LA PARISIENNE

## PÂTÉ CHAUD DE VEAU À LA PARISIENNE (Hot veal pie)

This pie can also be made with fillet of beef, lamb, duck, pheasant or other game. If using poultry or game half roast before making the pâté.

FOR THE PASTRY
12 oz. (3 cups) (340 g.) flour
7 tablespoons butter
1 tablespoon lard
2 eggs
½ cup water
salt

FILLING
1 lb. (454 g.) minced pork or
    sausagemeat
1 lb. (454 g.) finely sliced,
    beaten veal escalopes
½ lb. (227 g.) mushrooms,
    sliced
3 finely chopped shallots or
    1 small onion
3 tablespoons finely chopped
    parsley, tarragon and chervil
¼ pint (0.142 l.) white wine
½ cup brandy
4 thin slices raw ham
4 tablespoons butter
½ cup jellied consommé
salt and pepper

Make the pastry first by mixing the fat into the salt and flour, then adding one beaten egg and enough water to make a firm, pliable dough. Roll into a ball and chill until wanted. Butter an 8-inch mould, if possible one with spring sides, or if not available, a removable base. Marinate the flattened (paper-thin) slices of veal in the white wine and brandy with the herbs and chopped shallots for at least 1 hour, turning over during that time. Heat 2 tablespoons butter and very lightly soften the mushrooms, but on no account let them brown. Divide the pastry, keeping one third for the lid, roll out the larger part to the required size and line the mould. Coat the bottom and sides thinly with the sausagemeat, then pack the mould in layers of veal, ham, mushrooms and sausagemeat, seasoning each layer and leaving a little of the marinade. Do this until all those ingredients are finished, ending with a layer of sausagemeat. Pour over the remaining butter, melted. Dampen the edges of the pastry and put the remaining pastry on top, pressing down slightly and crimping the edges with a fork. Cut a slit on top, brush over with beaten egg, and bake in a hot oven (400°F.) for 15 minutes, then paint again with the egg and replace in a low oven (225°F.) for a further hour. If the top is getting too brown, then cover with foil. Meanwhile heat up the consommé with the marinade and boil down to at least half. Remove pie from mould and just before serving pour the consommé through the slit in the top with a small funnel. This pâté can also be served cold, when it will be a thick and delicious jelly.

Serves 6–8.

# SAUCE ESPAGNOLE

*Much of the fame of Montmartre cafés comes from the many celebrated painters who patronized them. Montmartre was like a country village in the nineteenth century and painters such as Delacroix, Géricault and Renoir patronized it because they were enchanted not only by its rusticity, but also the dark eyes, luminous skin and cherry lips of 'les petites de la Butte': one has only to think of the many Renoir paintings of these pretty girls to realize the impression they made. The tradition was carried on early in this century by Picasso, Utrillo, Derain, van Dongen and many others. See also pages 51 and 76.*

## SAUCE ESPAGNOLE OR SAUCE BRUNE

One of the classical, basic French brown sauces which makes the foundation for many other sauces such as: Madeira; Bordelaise; Lyonnaise; Piquante; Robert; and Italienne. This sauce keeps well in the refrigerator if boiled up at least once a week and put back in a clean screw-top jar, or it can be deep-frozen for future use. To make about 1 quart (1.142 l.) use the following amounts.

2 tablespoons good beef, veal
    or pork dripping or oil
4 tablespoons diced fat, salt
    pork or bacon
1 celery stalk, chopped
1 bayleaf
1 sprig thyme
2 sprigs parsley
2 medium diced carrots
1 medium sliced onion
2 tablespoons flour
salt and pepper
2 tablespoons tomato purée
3 pints (6 cups) (1.71 l.)
    brown stock or consommé
    at boiling point

Heat the dripping or oil, add the diced pork and vegetables and cook until they are golden, turning them so they cook evenly. Sprinkle the flour over, letting it cook for a few minutes until it is golden brown, then gradually add about half the boiling stock, whisking well with a wire whisk. When smooth add the herbs, then half the remaining stock, cover and simmer very slowly for about 2 hours or until the liquid is reduced to about half. Skim off any scum and fat. Stir in the tomato purée and the rest of the stock and season to taste. Cover and simmer again for about 20 minutes, scraping around the sides of the saucepan.

Strain through a fine sieve, pressing the juice from the vegetables, then leave to get cold and degrease completely. When cold refrigerate or freeze.

SAUCE RAGOÛT is made as above using poultry giblets and/or game bones and trimmings, and sometimes a little red wine is added. It is called SAUCE POIVRADE if the game has been marinated and a cup of marinade is added. If $\frac{1}{2}$ cup each of redcurrant jelly and cream is beaten into the Sauce Poivrade it is known as SAUCE VENAISON.

*Open-air café, place du Tertre, Montmartre, c.1904. Photographer, Eugène Atget.*

# COQUILLES SAINT-JACQUES AU VIN BLANC

This early film show was held in the 'Salon Indien' of the Grand Café, and the principal short films shown consisted of, a fire; a blacksmith at work; a baby having its lunch; fish swimming in bowl and a train arriving at a station. The brothers Auguste and Louis Lumière, inventors of the cinematograph, came from Lyons, and after experimenting for several years gave the first public showing of their films in 1895.

## COQUILLES SAINT-JACQUES AU VIN BLANC (Scallops with white wine)

| | |
|---|---|
| 8 large scallops | 2 tablespoons butter |
| 4 oz. (113 g.) streaky salt pork or unsmoked bacon | 2 glasses white wine |
| | 1 bayleaf |
| 2 shallots, finely chopped | 2 teaspoons finely chopped |
| pepper | parsley |
| 1 tablespoon flour | |

Dice the pork or bacon and trim and cut the scallops in bite-size pieces. Heat the butter and add the finely chopped shallots, the bayleaf and the diced pork and let them gently sauté until the shallots are pale yellow and the pork beginning to crisp up. Add the scallops, season with pepper and let them cook gently for about 7 minutes, stirring them all around meanwhile. Take the pork, shallots and scallops from the pan, removing the bayleaf, put them into a serving dish and keep warm. Then add the flour and white wine to the pan, mixing well with the pan juices, and let it reduce rapidly over a hot flame until the sauce is slightly syrupy. Finally add the chopped parsley and pour over the scallops. This can be put into individual scallop shells if wanted for a first course, sprinkled with breadcrumbs and heated in a hot oven (425°F.) for 10 minutes before serving.

Serves 8 for a first course or 4 for a main course.

*Audience leaving an early Lumière cinematograph projection at the Grand Café, 14 boulevard des Capucines, 1896.*

# PETITS MARCELLINS

'Fairs and festivals, it may be said, take the place of sport in France. There are fairs everywhere – miles upon miles of booths. Every fête day in summer has its fair. There are many things one can do for a penny: you do not realize the importance of a penny until you go to a fête . . . the air is thick with dust; flags and wreaths of paper flowers are stretched across the road . . . arrayed under awnings, decorated with crimson and gold are hundreds of cheap-jack stands . . . *"Un sou la fois, quatre chances pour un sou,"* cries a nasal voice. It is a lottery . . . there are roundabouts, weird and strange . . . in the middle are girls in tights and spangles, beating out the same old tune hour after hour. The roads are full of people, continually passing and repassing . . . absolutely happy with their merry-go-rounds, lotteries . . . shooting galleries . . . whole families sitting at the various tables – the mother and father with a huge bottle of wine . . . the children with a stack of *goffres* and other cakes.' Dorothy Menpes, *Paris*, 1909.

## PETITS MARCELLINS (Almond pastries)

Make pastry well in advance and chill.

1 egg
6 oz. (1½ cups) (170 g.) icing (confectioners') sugar
8 oz. (2 cups) (227 g.) sifted plain flour
4 tablespoons melted butter
1 tablespoon rum or Kirsch
icing sugar for garnish

FILLING

6 oz. (1½ cups) (170 g.) ground almonds
2 tablespoons Cointreau
6 oz. (⅔ cup) (170 g.) sugar
2 egg-yolks
8 oz. (1 cup) (226 g.) sugar
2 tablespoons flour
2 beaten egg-whites

Beat the egg and sifted icing sugar well, then add the melted butter, the rum or Kirsch and finally the flour. Mix until the pastry is firm and roll into a ball. Chill for several hours or overnight. Then roll out on a floured surface as thinly as possible, and cut into 3-inch circles, then put these into patty tins and prick the bottoms with a fork. To make the filling mix the ground almonds with the Cointreau and the 6 oz. sugar. Beat the egg-yolks until pale with the 8 oz. sugar, then combine the two mixtures and the flour, gradually. When well mixed fold in the stiffly beaten egg-whites. Fill the pastry cases with this, cover with a thick layer of icing (confectioners') sugar and bake in low to moderate (300–325°F.) preheated oven for about 30 minutes. The sugar top will harden in cooking, making a light crust.

Makes approx. 18 pastries.

*Fête de Montmartre, c.1862; La Butte before the construction of the church.*

# GIGOT AU PASTIS

*At the turn of the century Montparnasse was only a suburb of the* Quartier Latin *and the Luxembourg. The Dôme café was a small shack-like drinking place as early as 1898 : the Closerie des Lilas (which really was surrounded by lilacs) was a favourite café for writers (see page 59) ; the Rotonde, owned by le père Libion, opened around 1911, the year President Poincaré inaugurated the boulevard Raspail, and was a meeting-place for Russians such as Lenin, Trotsky and Ehrenburg; La Coupole opened in 1927, by which time the influx of Americans was considerable.*

Oliver Wendell Holmes, in *The Autocrat of the Breakfast-Table* quotes Thomas Appleton: 'Good Americans, when they die, go to Paris'; although Roger Wild said, 'Montparnasse . . . was too often a matter of pox, clap, itch, fleas, filth and hunger.'

## GIGOT AU PASTIS (Leg of Lamb with pastis)

Pastis is the generic name for aniseed-based spirits such as Pernod, anise etc. Recipe kindly given by Monique Guillaume.

4 lb. (approx. 2 kg.) leg of lamb
2 cloves garlic
a few sprigs rosemary
1 sprig thyme
3 tablespoons olive oil
1 glass ($\frac{1}{2}$ cup) pastis
salt and pepper

FOR THE SAUCE
1$\frac{1}{2}$ lb. (681 g.) peeled tomatoes, fresh or canned
1 medium sliced onion
1 sliced shallot
1 bayleaf
1 lump sugar
2 tablespoons olive oil

Make several slits in the leg and insert slivers of peeled garlic. Put into a baking tin and smear with the oil and sprinkle with the chopped rosemary and thyme. (If preferred the lamb can be boned and rolled with the herbs inside: this method makes carving much easier.) Roast in a moderate to hot oven (375°F.), or on a spit, allowing 15 minutes per pound and 15 minutes over, for rare, and 20–25 minutes for well-done meat. Add salt and pepper during cooking. While the meat is roasting make the sauce by heating the oil and sautéeing the onion and shallot. Then add all the other ingredients, stir and cook without the lid for 20–30 minutes. Before serving remove the bayleaf.

Put the meat on a warmed serving dish, defat the pan juices, put into a gravy boat, and just before serving, or at table, warm the pastis in a ladle, pour over the lamb and set alight. Serve rice or pasta separately.

Serves 6–8.

*The poet Paul Verlaine (1844–96) drinking absinthe in Montparnasse, possibly La Closerie des Lilas, c.1891.*

# LAPIN AUX PRUNEAUX

*'. . . the corncrake . . . the woodcock, the partridge, the pheasant, the rabbit, and the hare; this is game in the proper sense of the term – ground game and marsh game, furry game and feathered game . . . Game is one of our favourite foods, being wholesome, tasty, full-flavoured and easily digestible by all except the aged.'*
*Brillat-Savarin*, La Physiologie du Goût, *1825*.

## LAPIN AUX PRUNEAUX (Rabbit with prunes)

Also excellent for hare, but cooking time must be increased by half an hour.

Rabbit and hare should be hung for at least three days in a cool place before skinning, gutting, and cooking. The day before it is needed, soak for 3–4 hours in salt and cold water, turning at least once. Then leave overnight in a marinade consisting of: ½ cup oil, 3 tablespoons wine vinegar (or red or white wine), 1 sliced onion or shallot, a bayleaf, 6 allspice, a sprig of rosemary, black peppercorns and a little salt. Turn the rabbit or hare over during marinating time so that it absorbs the marinade.

| | |
|---|---|
| 1 young* rabbit or hare, jointed | 2 tablespoons oil |
| ½ pint (1 cup) (0.285 l.) red wine | 2 tablespoons butter |
| 3 medium sliced carrots | 2 cloves chopped garlic |
| 1 large sliced onion | ½ lb. (227 g.) soaked prunes |
| ¼ pint (½ cup) (0.142 l.) marinade | 4 rashers bacon |
| 2 tablespoons flour | pinch of marjoram |
| | salt and freshly ground pepper |

*The animal is young if the ear splits easily when torn.

Lift the rabbit from the marinade and pat it dry. Heat the oil, butter and bacon, letting the bacon brown, then sauté the rabbit all over, in an ovenproof casserole. Strain the prunes and remove pits. Add the sliced vegetables to the rabbit and let them sauté lightly. Shake the flour over, and turn the rabbit, letting the flour brown slightly. Then add the wine, and the marinade. Let it bubble up, then add the bayleaf from the marinade, the marjoram, prunes, garlic and seasonings. Let it come to the boil, cover and transfer to a moderate oven (350°F.) for about 1½ hours, or until the legs are quite tender when lightly pricked with a fork. Continue cooking time for at least a half an hour if using hare. Serve with hot red cabbage (page 6) and redcurrant jelly. This dish can be made the day before it is needed, for it will only improve with reheating.

Serves 3–4.

Marquise de Valromey's CIVET DE LIÈVRE (Hare in wine). (Reserve ¼ pint (½ cup) (0.142 l.) blood from the hare.)

After marinating as above: Chop an onion and a little under 1 oz. (28 g.) fat pork and put them with 2 oz. (57 g.) butter into an earthenware or iron pot. Add the jointed hare and cook 20 minutes; sprinkle over 1 oz. (28 g.) flour; stir and cook slowly for twenty-five minutes. Put in a soup ladle of beef stock and the same of good red wine. Season and cook for a further thirty-five minutes. Mash the cooked liver to a fine paste: add the strained marinade and the blood of the hare. Put through a sieve and five minutes before serving add to the hare and bring to the boil. Add a few drops of vinegar and finally a spoonful of olive oil.

103

*Poultry and game stall, Les Halles market, 1900. Photographer, Eugène Atget.*

# PARFAIT AU CHOCOLAT

After the Great Exhibition of 1851 in England, the first of its kind to be held, Louis Napoleon (who had visited it at Queen Victoria and Prince Albert's invitation) was quick to realize that here was a way to show the world his power, also that Paris and France could compete with London. In 1853 Baron Georges Haussmann was given a free hand and in a few years was to transform Paris, not always to everyone's liking. Most guests from all over Europe to the Universal Exhibition of 1855 arrived at the Gare de l'Est (then called Strasbourg): the Gare du Nord was just completed but the approaches were still rubble, so they were driven down the new boulevard de Strasbourg. Queen Victoria in a letter to the King of the Belgians from Saint-Cloud in August 1855, wrote: 'I am delighted, enchanted, amused and interested, and I think I never saw anything more beautiful and gay than Paris . . . They have asked to call a new street, which we opened, after me!' (Avenue Victoria parallel to the embankment and rue de Rivoli, into the place de l'Hôtel de Ville.) These exhibitions became a French feature, occurring every few years: in the 1867 Exhibition each country had its own national restaurant, the Buffet Anglais proving a great success. The Goncourt brothers thought the barmaids looked like 'prostitutes of the Apocalypse, a mixture of clowns and beasts: splendid disquieting animals'.

The Eiffel Tower was built for the 1889 Exhibition, the possibility of its erection causing an outcry from writers such as Maupassant, Sardou, and Dumas fils. It was supposed to be demolished in 1909, but it remains today, a Paris landmark.

Slater's, the London caterers (see left of photograph), and Chocolat Menier, both of whom survive today, were among the many exhibitors.

## PARFAIT AU CHOCOLAT (Chocolate parfait)

| | |
|---|---|
| ½ lb. (227 g.) Chocolat Menier or other bitter chocolate | 2 tablespoons butter |
| | 2 tablespoons brandy, rum or black coffee |
| 4 large eggs, separated | |

Heat the chocolate and butter either over hot water, or on a very low heat in a thick saucepan, stirring well until it is melted. Remove from the heat and add the brandy or coffee gradually, mixing thoroughly. One by one stir in the egg-yolks and beat well. Put into small individual cups, and leave overnight in a cold place. This is very rich and has a much better flavour than the ordinary chocolate mousse. However, if that is preferred, then stiffly beat the egg-whites and add them before putting into the pots.

Serves 4–6.

*Paris Exhibition 1900, with Jena Bridge, Eiffel Tower, and Chaillot Palace in background.*

# PORC À LA NORMANDE

The iron grilles on the ground-floor windows mean that this was an estaminet (a name in former times for cafés where patrons were allowed to smoke: nowadays it usually means a café or restaurant entirely open to the street); in the eighteenth century all places of this kind were required by law to have these grilles to prevent customers from leaping out if the police dropped in unexpectedly.

The cider, perry and Calvados (apple brandy) advertised outside the café undoubtedly mean that the owner was either of Breton or of Norman stock. Norman custom demands that the diner takes un trou Normand, or a glass of Calvados, between courses to act as a digestif: 'bouillon, and pot-au-feu, after which a glass of wine is taken; then tripe; then leg of mutton. Here a halt is called for the trou Normand. We fall to again with roast veal, then fowl, then the desserts, coffee and again Calvados'. Curnonsky (Maurice-Edmond Sailland), 1924.

## PORC À LA NORMANDE (roast pork, Norman style)

4 lb. (2 kg.) loin or leg pork
12 small apples, cored but unpeeled
3 sage leaves
1 pint (2 cups) (0.57 l.) cider
salt and freshly ground pepper
3 large onions
1 teaspoon each: grated nutmeg and cinnamon
1 glass Calvados

Put the pork (fat side up) into a roasting pan with the onions cut into 4 and a fraction of each sage leaf on top of them. Season and pour round the cider, then roast in a moderate to hot oven (400°F.) for ½ hour. Lower the heat and roast for 30 minutes to the pound, basting with the hot stock from time to time. After the meat has been cooking for about 1 hour add the unpeeled but cored apples to the pan around the pork, each one heavily sprinkled inside with nutmeg and cinnamon. When the meat is cooked, remove to a warmed serving dish, arrange the apples and onions around it, and keep warm. Reduce the pan juices on top of the stove, and warm the Calvados. Set it alight and add to the gravy. Ladle out several spoonfuls and pour over the meat and fruit, then serve the remainder in a sauce boat. If preferred the Calvados can be warmed, then poured over the meat and ignited, before serving. The cider stock will make the pork crackling very crisp and crunchy.

Serves 8–10.

Restaurant 'Au Bourdon', 64 rue de Varenne, c.1898.

# SOUFFLÉ DE CRABE

*This early café was frequented by the artists from the neighbouring Théâtre Lyrique and the Théâtre Imperial de Cirque. The boulevard du Temple is still renowned for its spectacles and has been called 'une foire perpetuelle', the perpetual fair, including a circus, La Gaité Lyrique, Folies-Dramatiques, les Funambules as well as many cafés and restaurants. There is today a Restaurant des Artistes in the rue Lepic, which is famous for its hare pâté, and turbot soufflé which is baked directly on the plate it is served from, not in a dish. This golden masterpiece is the result of years of experiment by the Caillon family.*

## SOUFFLÉ DE CRABE (Crab soufflé)
Lobster, crawfish, salmon etc. can also be used.

2 oz. (¼ cup) (57 g.) butter
3 tablespoons flour
scant ½ pint (1 cup) (0.285 l.) hot milk
salt and freshly ground pepper
pinch cayenne pepper
squeeze of lemon juice

½ lb. (1 cup) (227 g.) shredded crabmeat
2 tablespoons brandy
2 tablespoons heavy cream
½ lb. whole pieces crab
4 beaten egg-yolks
5 egg-whites, beaten stiff but not dry

Well butter a 4-pint (8 cups) (2 l.) soufflé dish. Then melt the butter slowly, add the flour and cook for about 1 minute. Take off the heat and stir in the scant ½ pint milk and season to taste. Put back on the heat, and stirring all the time cook until sauce is thick and smooth. Cool slightly, then add the squeeze of lemon: mix the shredded crabmeat with the brandy and add to the basic mixture. Take one third of this mixture and mix with the heavy cream then put this on the bottom of the prepared soufflé dish. Cover this with the whole pieces of crab. Add the beaten egg-yolks slowly to the remaining basic mixture, stirring well, and finally add the beaten egg-whites. Put this on top of the crabmeat in the dish, and bake in a moderate oven (375°F.) for 40–50 minutes. The sauce at the bottom should be spooned up with the soufflé when serving.

Serves 4–6. If liked this mixture can be divided among 6 small individual soufflé dishes.

If cornflour (cornstarch) is used instead of flour this soufflé can be cooked ahead of time and reheated and repuffed, as follows: leave in the dish or dishes, and when needed, set in a shallow pan with 1 inch of hot water. Put into a moderate oven (350°F.) for about ½ hour.

*Café des Artistes, boulevard du Temple, c.1850s.*

# SAVARIN DE MÉNAGE

'Pictures here are very cheap. You can purchase plenty at one or two *sous* each on the different quays. Nine out of ten are portraits of Napoleon . . . the ladies not only have their portraits painted, but paint their own faces also. . . .' G. W. M. Reynolds, *Pickwick Abroad or the Tour in France*, 1839.

After a stroll in the May sunshine on the *quai*, coffee and cake at a nearby café are a pleasant way to pass the time.

## SAVARIN DE MÉNAGE

Savarin (originally called Brillat-Savarin, the invention of M. Julien in 1840) dough is made with yeast in pastryshops: this is a quick and simple method for housewives. The cylindrical-shaped, small Babas are made the same way with raisins added.

'The cakes were of three kinds – Babas, Madeleines, and Savarins – three sous apiece, fourpence-halfpenny the set of three. No nicer cakes are made in France. . . . You must begin with the Madeleine . . . then the Baba; and finish up with the Savarin, which is shaped like a ring, very light, and flavoured with rum. And then you must really leave off.' George du Maurier, *Trilby*, 1894.

3 oz. (barely 1 cup) (85 g.) sifted flour
2 eggs
4 oz. (1 cup) (113 g.) sugar
1 teaspoon baking powder
pinch of salt

FOR THE SYRUP
6 tablespoons rum
2 tablespoons hot water
4 tablespoons sugar

Butter a ring-mould and preheat the oven to 325°F. Heat the mixing bowl by rinsing with very hot water, and wrap the base of the bowl in a hot towel. Beat the eggs until doubled in size, then combine all dry ingredients and fold them in gradually, beating well all the time. Put into the prepared mould, so that the mixture comes to half-way up. Bake in the centre of the oven for 20 minutes, then increase the heat to 400°F. and cook for 10 minutes longer. Put on to a wire rack, cover with a towel and leave for 5 minutes. Then invert on to the serving plate and prick all over, lightly, with a fork. Heat the syrup ingredients slowly until the sugar dissolves, and it is below boiling point, otherwise the rum will lose its alcoholic content. Spoon over the cake and leave for at least 1 hour. Serve plain, with Crème Chantilly (page 87), or mix the Chantilly with chopped crystallized fruits and put into the middle of the cake.

Serves 4–6.

For Madeleines, see page 85.

*The Quai d'Orsay, May 1898. Photographer, Eugène Atget.*

# CROISSANTS

Although croissants are now an accepted part of French life, they in fact originated in Budapest in 1686 in the following way. That year the Turks were besieging the city and in order to reach the centre of the town unobserved they had tunnelled underground. Bakers working during the night heard the noise, gave the alarm and the city was saved. To commemorate this victory the bakers were allowed to make a special cake in the form of a crescent, the emblem which decorates the Ottoman flag.

## CROISSANTS

1 tablespoon butter
1 teaspoon salt
1½ tablespoons sugar
½ pint (1 cup) (0.285 l.) warm scalded milk
1 oz. (28 g.) (1 packet) yeast dissolved in 4 tablespoons tepid water

1 lb. (4 cups) (454 g.) flour
½ lb. (1 cup) (227 g.) butter
1 egg-yolk for glazing, mixed with 2 tablespoons milk

Put the butter, salt and sugar from the first column into a mixing bowl, pour over the scalded milk, mix lightly and leave until lukewarm. Dissolve the yeast in the tepid water, add and stir lightly. Add the flour and knead well, until the dough is firm and elastic. Cover and leave in a warm place until doubled in size (or put into a polythene bag and leave) for about 1 hour. Knead for 1 minute, then chill the dough in the refrigerator for 2 hours. Roll out the chilled dough into a strip three times as long as it is wide. Spread the butter (in 2nd column) over the dough and fold the ends of the strip in toward the centre, envelope fashion. Turn the dough half round and roll across it. Chill for ½ hour, then repeat this operation twice more, the last time leaving the dough in the refrigerator for 1 hour. It is then ready for use.

Roll out the dough to a ¼-inch thickness and cut into 4-inch squares. Divide each square into 2 triangles and starting with the longest side, roll each triangle towards the point, so that the pointed end will be in the middle. Bend slightly into crescents, brush with the egg and milk mixture and put onto an unbuttered baking tray. Bake for 15–20 minutes in a moderate oven (375°F.), but if they are not wanted at once, keep the uncooked croissants in the fridge.

Makes about 20.

*Group drinking outside a café, rue Pascal, c.1852.*

# CROQUE MONSIEUR

*Billiards were an added attraction in many cafés, but a law was passed in 1895 restricting them, for it was found that quite a lively trade went on involving substantial sums of money with very experienced players rooking the amateurs.*

## CROQUE MONSIEUR

A delicious hot snack when properly made: too often it is just ham and toasted cheese in Paris today.

| | |
|---|---|
| 4 thick slices white bread | 2 tablespoons butter |
| 4 oz. (113 g.) cheese, preferably Swiss | 1 tablespoon butter |
| | 2 teaspoons flour |
| 2 thick slices cooked ham | 1 cup creamy milk, warmed |
| 1 egg, beaten | pepper |

Trim the crusts from the bread, grate the cheese, setting aside 2 tablespoons of it. Put a slice of ham on 2 of the bread slices, then press the remaining grated cheese on top of the ham. Make a sandwich by putting another slice of bread on top and press down. Heat up the tablespoon of butter, then stir in the flour and let it cook for a minute, then add the warm milk and stir until it is thick and smooth. Add the 2 tablespoons grated cheese and pepper to taste. Keep warm, but not boiling. Beat the egg and dip the two sandwiches into it turning them gently so that both sides are soaked with the egg. Heat up the 2 tablespoons butter and fry the sandwiches until golden and crisp on both sides. Serve with the creamy cheese sauce over the top.

Enough for 2.

Croque Monsieur can also be made in the form of open sandwiches, in which case first fry the egg-soaked bread in the butter, put the ham and cheese on top and lightly grill the cheese so that it melts but does not colour. Then serve with the cheese sauce over all.

*Café and billiard rooms, corner of the rue de Plâtre, 1852. Photographer Charles Marville.*

# JAMBON AUX PRUNES

The column with Napoleon I on top in the Place Vendôme was pulled down in May 1871 by the painter, Gustave Courbet (then president of the Commission of Fine Arts) and his supporters for both aesthetic and political reasons. After the fall of the Commune he was imprisoned, heavily fined, and spent some time in exile. While the first Communist revolution in the world was taking place Edmond de Goncourt wrote in his Journal: 'It is really ironical to see Parisians, of all people those who most like their meat fresh and their vegetables new – consulting one another in front of the tinned provisions of cosmopolitan grocers'. '. . . the tenderness, I might almost say with which people handle 4 pound loaves – those fine white loaves of which Paris has been so long deprived.' 28th February 1871.

The canning process was invented by the Appert brothers, Nicholas and François, in 1809 after the French Government had offered a 12,000-franc prize for the discovery of a practical method of preserving food. It was perfected by François and canned food was used by Napoleon for his armies in the attack on Russia. In 1810 a patent of the Appert method was taken out in England and later in the United States. In 1823 the Americans Underwood and Kensett set up commercial canneries in Boston and New York. However, in 1839 an Englishman, Peter Durand, conceived and patented the prototype of the tin-plated container.

## JAMBON AUX PRUNES (Ham with Plums)

3 lb. (approx. 1½ kg.) cooked or canned ham

2 cans red plums, approx. 15 oz. (426 g.) each

1 tablespoon cornflour (cornstarch)

¾ pint (1½ cups) (approx. ½ l.) red wine

2 tablespoons honey or brown sugar

pepper

Drain the juice from the plums and remove the stones. Put the ham removed from the tin into an ovenproof dish, pour over the wine and put the plums around. Spread the honey or sugar on top of the ham, cover, and bake for ¾ hour in a moderate oven (350°F.). Put the ham on a warm serving plate, cream the cornflour with a little water, then add to the pan juices, stirring all the time until it is smooth. Season to taste, then pour the sauce over the ham and garnish with parsley. The ham can be sliced first if preferred.

Serves 6–8.

*Courbet congratulates the sailors who have demolished the Vendôme column during the Commune, 1871.*

# ŒUFS BROUILLÉS À L'ORANGE

*The French have been pioneers in ballooning since the fire balloon of the Montgolfier brothers reached a height of 1½ miles at Annonay in 1783 and again at Versailles later in the year, the first aerial passengers being a sheep, a duck and a cock. In November the same year Jean Pilâtre de Rozier and the Marquis d'Arlandes made the first free balloon ascent from the Bois de Boulogne. Also in 1783 J. A. C. Charles ascended from the Champ de Mars in a balloon inflated with hydrogen gas and many features of modern balloons stem from his inventions. Balloons were first used by the French military during the Revolutionary wars and also during the Siege of Paris, see page 17.*

## ŒUFS BROUILLÉS À L'ORANGE
(Scrambled eggs with orange)

If served in washed, scraped half-shells of orange peel it makes a pretty first course (either hot or cold*) or a light meal.

8 eggs
finely grated rind 1 orange
either 8 rounds toast or 4
   oranges cut in half, the
   pulp removed, the shells
   washed.

8 tablespoons cream
1 tablespoon white vermouth
1½ tablespoons butter
salt and pepper

Finely grate the peel of 1 orange, then beat the eggs lightly with a fork and add three-quarters of the peel, the cream, vermouth and seasonings. Melt the butter in a heavy (or a non-stick) saucepan and when just golden and foaming add the egg mixture, stirring constantly on a low heat. Stir until they are creamy and slightly runny on top (a few minutes only) as the heat will continue the cooking and they will be overcooked if left until dry. Serve either on the toast or in the orange shells with the remaining grated peel on top.

   Serves 2–4.

\* If serving cold cover the top with a thin layer of aspic made according to directions on the packet.

*Captive Balloon, Trocadèro, c.1890s.*

# INDEX